A Scriptural Thesis
on
Water
Baptism

by Kevin J. Conner

CONNER
MINISTRIES

CONNER
MINISTRIES

Published by Conner Ministries Inc

Cover Design by Mark Conner
WEB: kevinconner.org
Email: kevin.conner321@gmail.com
Visit www.amazon.com for a list of
other books by Kevin Conner available on Kindle.

About this Book

This is a thesis written for one of the author's degrees. Here the author treats thoroughly the Bible view of water baptism with a very interesting and challenging section on the Name of God and its involvement in baptism.

Submitted in partial fulfilment towards a Bachelor of Theology Degree at International Bible College (San Antonio, Taxes. 78228) in 1973.

About the Author

Kevin John Conner is recognized internationally as a teaching-apostle after many years in both church and Bible College ministry. He has written many textbooks used by ministers and students throughout the world. He has been in great demand as a teacher and has travelled extensively. Kevin lives in Melbourne, Australia with his wife Rene.

TABLE OF CONTENTS

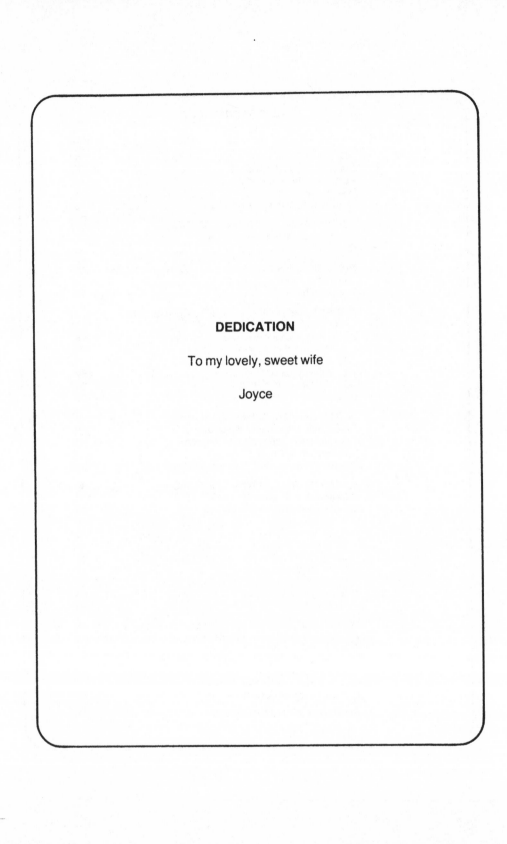

DEDICATION

To my lovely, sweet wife

Joyce

INTRODUCTION

The Word of God has foretold that in the Last Days the Holy Spirit would be poured out upon all flesh. [1]

It is absolutely evident, to those who have eyes to see and ears to hear, and hearts to perceive, that the Church is living in the last of the Last Days, for the Holy Spirit is being poured out upon every kindred, tongue, tribe and nation.

With the outpouring of the Spirit upon all flesh, there has come a renewed emphasis on the Word of God. This is as it should be, for the ministry of the Holy Spirit is to quicken, energize, and illuminate the Word of God. "The Letter killeth, but the Spirit giveth life."[2] The Spirit is the life of the Letter.

One of the great facets of truth in God's Word is that which pertains to the subject of Baptism: whether it be concerning the Baptism in or with the Holy Spirit, or Baptism into the Body of Christ, or Baptism in Water. The whole subject of Baptism is coming into focus more and more. It seems as if that which took place in the house of Cornelius under the ministry of the Apostle Peter is taking place once again; for, as Peter was preaching the Word of the Gospel, the Holy Spirit fell on the Gentiles who heard the Word, for they began to speak with other tongues as the Spirit gave them utterance. [3]

When Peter recognized that God had baptized the Gentiles in the Holy Spirit, he commanded them to be baptized in water. [4] The order here was the exception, not the general rule, in the Book of Acts, because other records show Water Baptism preceding Holy Spirit Baptism.

A repetition of this is taking place today in the main-line Denominations and untold numbers of believers are being baptized in the Holy Spirit.

---

[1] Thompson, Frank Charles, The New Chain Reference Bible, B. B. Kirkbride Bible Co., Inc., Indianapolis, Indiana, 1964. Acts 2:17.

[2] *Ibid,* II Corithians 3:6.

[3] *Ibid,* Acts 10:44-46.

[4] *Ibid,* Acts 10:47-48.

However, the question of Water Baptism has to be faced. Is the order that took place in the house of Cornelius a valid order today for those who have had the like experience?

It is self-evident that the Spirit of God is challenging the Church as to the truth of Baptism, and will continue to focus in on all who desire to "make all things according to the pattern" [5] as laid down in the Word of God for the establishment of the principles and practices of a New Testament Church in our day.

The Lord has purposed that He will build His Church according to His own will and plan, and each member of that Church must measure up to the Divine standard set forth in the Holy Scriptures.

All capital letters and underline throughout this thesis are for the purpose of the emphasis the Author wishes to make.

Kevin John Conner
Author

---

[5] Thompson, Hebrews 8:5.

STATEMENT OF THE PROBLEM

The Doctrine of Baptisms has been, and still is in many Theological areas, a great field of truth presenting a number of problems. These problems basically center around the Interpretation of Baptism as an Ordinance, as to Form or Mode and also around the words of a Formula to be used in the administration of this Rite.

Some Denominations believe that a person is not born again until Baptism. Others believe Water Baptism is simply an outward sign of an inward experience. Some teach Infant Baptism is a sure guarantee of salvation. All of these things involve that which pertains to a proper **Interpretation** of Baptism.

In other areas questions arise as to Form or Mode. Is Baptism by sprinkling or immersion? Here it is not the **fact** but the **Mode** of Baptism that is in question.

The problem moves beyond these things into the area of **Formula**, or what particular words, if any, are to be used in administration. Should a person be baptized "in the Name of the Father, and of the Son, and of the Holy Ghost" according to the Command of Jesus in Matthew's Gospel? [6] Or should a person be baptized in the Name of the Lord Jesus Christ as set forth in the Book of Acts? [7] Or, should it be both?

Thus we have presented before us a number of vital questions, which demand an answer. Is Water Baptism necessary to salvation? Is it a means of grace? Is it to be by sprinkling or immersion? Is Infant Baptism taught in the Scripture? What is the Mode and what is the Formula for Baptism? Is it all a matter of obedience in order that the candidate may have the answer of a clear conscience before God?

Do words even matter as long as the condition of the heart is right before the Lord?

Therefore to summarize and define the problem, we ask: "What is the proper Scriptural answer, and what is the Apostolic interpretation of the Ordinance of Baptism in all its related areas?

This is the statement of the problem.

[6.] Thompson, Matthew 28:19
[7.] *Ibid,* Acts 2:36,38

PURPOSE OF THE STUDY

THE PURPOSE of this study is to explore and research the given problem, and find out what is the real meaning of Baptism, and what is the proper interpretation of this Ordinance with all of its relative questions.

In these days of Charismatic Renewal, when God is pouring out His Spirit upon all flesh, regardless of Religious Denomination or Organizational background, there has arisen a fresh interest in the subject of Baptism, or "The Doctrine of Baptisms". [8]

Because of this renewed emphasis by the Spirit of God on the Doctrine of Baptisms, spoken of in the Epistle to the Hebrews, and the 'One Baptism' [9] spoken of by Paul in the Epistle to the Ephesians, it becomes a challenge and necessity to explore that which God has revealed concerning this subject.

The ultimate purpose is to bring the believer back to the Holy Scriptures, the final 'Court of Appeal', the final authority, for all Christian Faith and Practice, and into an experiential knowledge of this great truth. "What saith the Scripture?" [10]

Here then is the purpose of this study.

---

[8] Thompson, Hebrews 6:2
[9] *Ibid,* Ephesians 4:5
[10] *Ibid,* Galatians 4:30

HISTORY OF THE PROBLEM

Church History, both Early and Modern, abound with evidences of the great controversy over Baptism.

The Church, for centuries, has been torn and rent asunder into numerous divisions and heresies over the subject. Even the Church at Corinth in Apostolic times was torn by party-spirit and sectarianism over personalities in regard to Baptism. Paul writes to them concerning the divisions among them with the words: "Is Christ divided? was Paul crucified for you? or were ye baptized in the name of Paul? I thank God that I baptized none of you but Crispus and Gaius, lest any should say that I had baptized in mine own name."[11]

The Denominational divisions in Christendom today give abundant testimony of the reaction to and attitude over Baptism in Modern Times.

Various Denominations reject Baptism in any form, totally refusing to believe or accept that part of Divine Revelation, relegating it to the inauguration of the Early Church, or spiritualizing it out of actual practice.

Other Organizations have been torn asunder over Modes, Formulas and Interpretations of Baptism, until there exists numerous Sects which believe in Baptism but are divided as to its administration.

Many times believers see a part or fragment of truth, assuming it to be the whole, when, if all the fragments were put together, then the whole would be seen as God intended it to be seen. The Blessed Holy Spirit is the inspirer and illuminator of the Word of God and it is only as the Christian is enlightened by the Spirit that the Church as a whole will come into the unity of that faith which was "once delivered to the saints". [12]

The Holy Spirit does not contradict the Word He inspired, nor does He give contradictory or partial interpretation of that Word.

He knows exactly what was meant when it was written under His influence, and as the believer allows the Word-Inspirer to quicken and interpret, then will come that full understanding of Divinely given Ordinances.

[11.] Thompson, 1Corinthians 1:13-15
[12.] *Ibid,* Jude 3

ORGANIZATION OF THE THESIS

This study endeavors to set forth the principles of interpretation of the New Testament Scriptures related to the subject of Water Baptism, as understood by the Early Church in Apostolic Times.

The thesis is organized in the following manner:

The Bibliography lists the works quoted or researched as pertaining to the subject matter.

CHAPTER 2:

DEFINITION OF THE TERM "BAPTISM"

In the beginning of a thesis on the subject of Baptism, it is necessary that the meaning of the word be defined. Terminology and definition of words is a pre-requisite to a clearer and fuller understanding. This Section deals with the Greek usage of the word, both Classical and Koine Greek, as in New Testament times.

GREEK CLASSICAL USAGE OF THE TERM

The Greek word βαπτιζω (Baptizo) is the word used in records in the New Testament when speaking of Baptism, whether it pertains to Baptism in Water or Baptism in the Holy Spirit. The true meaning of the Greek word βαπτιζω , "to baptize", is immersion. The term was well established in Classical Greek simply to mean "to immerse, to plunge under."

It is generally accepted that the Greek word βαπτιζω is derived from the word βαπτω (Bapto). This word is still preserved and appears often in the Old Testament.

Prince [12] tells us in relation to this that the Greek word βαπτω is used three times in the New Testament and it is translated as 'dip'. The rich man in Hades desired that Lazarus would come and 'dip' the tip of his finger in water and cool his tongue as he was tormented in the flame. Jesus 'dipped' the sop before He gave the Judas the betrayer. And then again, the Lord Jesus comes again the second time clothed with a garment 'dipped' in blood. Each of these Scriptures use the same Greek word βαπτω which means "to dip something into a fluid, and then take it out again." See Luke's Gospel, and John's Gospel and Revelation. [13] Prince [14] also shows that the Greek word εμβαπτω (empbapto) is used three times in the New Testament, from which the word 'Baptize comes. The three references are found

---

[12] Prince, Derek, **From Jordan to Pentecost**, p.10,11
[13] Thompson, Luke 16:24; John 13:26; Revelation 19:13
[14] Prince, Derek, **From Jordan to Pentecost**, p.10,11

in Matthew, Mark and John. [15] Again it has the same meaning as 'bapto', that is, "to dip." Thus 'bapto' and 'empbapto' give the same meaning and from these words 'Baptize' is derived.

Strong [16] confirms the same in his Greek Dictionary of the New Testament, when he says that the word means "to whelm", i.e., cover wholly with fluid; in the New Testament only in a qualified special sense. And again, i.e., (lit.) to moisten (a part of ones body), as (by implication) to stain (as with a dye): — dip.

So also Gerhard Kittel [17] says that the word $\beta\alpha\pi\tau\omega$ (bapto) means "to dip in water", "to dye", and is used by Josephus only in this sense, while the word $\beta\alpha\mu\mu\alpha$ (bamma) speaks of "dyed material", and $\beta\alpha\pi\tau\alpha$ (bapta) of "dyed or coloured clothes." Kittel continues to show that the word $\beta\alpha\pi\tau\iota\zeta\omega$ occurs in the sense of "to immerse", and is translated as such from the time of Hippocrates, and in Plato, and especially the later writers of Classical literature. These later writers also using the word with the meaning of "to sink" (in the mud), "to suffer shipwreck", "to drown, to perish."

In the fourth or fifth Century B.C., 'Baptizo' was used by PLATO of a young man "overwhelmed" by clever philosophical arguments. [18] The writing of HIPPOCRATES, in or about the fourth Century B.C., used 'Baptizo' of people being "submerged" in water, and of sponges being "dipped" in water. [19] Even the Septuagint (Greek Translation of the Old Testament) used 'Baptizo' to translate the passage found in First Kings Chapter 5 and verse 14, where Naaman "dipped" himself seven times in Jordan. [20]

Coming down to the second Century B.C., 'Baptizo' is used by STRABO to describe people who could not swim as being "submerged" beneath the surface of the water (in specific contrast to logs of wood floating on the surface). [21]

---

[15] Thompson, Matthew 26:23; Mark 14:20; John 13:26b

[16] Strong, Augustus Hopkins, **Exhaustive Concordance**, Greek Dict., 911

[17] Kittel, Gerhard, **Theological Dictionary of the New Testament**, p.529

[18] Prince, Derek, **From Jordan to Pentecost**, p.12

[19] *Ibid.* p.12

[20] *Ibid.* p.13

[21] Prince, Derek, **From Jordan to Pentecost**, p.13

Then again, in the first Century A.D., JOSEPHUS, the famous Jewish historian, metaphorically used 'Baptizo' to describe a man "plunging" a sword into his own neck, and of the City of Jerusalem being "overwhelmed" or "plunged" to irremediable destruction by internal strife. [22]

The testimony of Classical Greek unquestionably shows that the meaning of the word 'bapto' is "to dip, to immerse", or "to plunge under", as in the bathing of oneself, or the dyeing of a garment, or other materials.

GREEK KOINE USAGE OF THE TERM

The word 'Koine' simply means 'Common', and was the Greek language that prevailed from about 300 B.C., to the close of the ancient history about A.D. 500. The New Testament was written within this Koine period, thus giving us the Biblical or Jewish Greek.

The evidence on hand shows also that the Greek word 'Baptizo' which has its descent from 'bapto' still holds the same meaning, but takes on a fuller significance in the light of the New Testament. Throughout the different stages and changes of the Greek language, the term has survived in Modern Greek to still mean the same; "to immerse, to plunge under."

W. E. Vine, on the word $\beta\alpha\pi\tau\iota\sigma\mu\alpha$ (Baptisma) states, "baptism, consisting of the processes of immersion, submersion, and emergence (from bapto, to dip), is used of (a) John's Baptism; (b) of Christian Baptism; (c) of the overwhelming afflictions and judgments to which the Lord voluntarily submitted on the Cross, i.e., Luke 12:50; (d) of the sufferings of His followers which they would experience, not of a vicarious character, but in fellowship with the sufferings of their Master. [23]

Vine continues and he interprets $\beta\alpha\pi\tau\iota\sigma\mu\sigma\varsigma$ (Baptismos) as distinct from $\beta\alpha\pi\tau\iota\sigma\mu\alpha$ (Baptisma, the ordinance), and is used of the ceremonial washings of articles in Mark Chapter 7 and verses 4 and 8, in some texts, and Hebrews Chapter 9 verse 10, and once in a general

---

[22] *Ibid*, p.13

[23] Vine, W. E., **Expository Dictionary of New Testament Words**, p.69,97

sense, in Hebrews Chapter 6 and verse 2. [24]

On the verb βαπτιζω (Baptizo), "to baptize", he also writes that this verb, primarily a frequentative form of 'bapto' (to dip) was used among the Greeks to signify the dyeing of a garment, or the drawing of water by dipping a vessel into another, etc. [25]

Arndt and Gingrich confirm the same thing, that the word βαπτιζω (Baptizo) means "to dip, immerse, dip oneself, wash" (in non-Christian Lit.), also, "plunge, sink, drench, overwhelm, etc.," in our literature only in ritual sense. [26]

Strong's notes on the word 'Baptizo' (βαπτιζω) defines its meaning as "to make overwhelmed" (i.e., fully wet), used only (in the New Testament) of ceremonial ablutions, especially (technically) of the ordinance of Christian Baptism. [27]

Kittel comments on this word also, and shows that Baptism is "immersion". He further shows that even βαπτισμος used to be regarded as a new Jewish and Christian term. The Levitical "cleansings" of vessels or of the body is shown by the Greek word βαπτισμοι , as used in Mark Chapter 7 and verse 4, and Hebrews Chapter 9 and verse 10. Kittel goes on to explain further that βαπτισμα is the specific New Testament word used for 'Baptism', being used of John's Baptism as well as Christian Baptism. [28]

Liddell & Scott define βαπτιζω as "dip, plunge". [29]

Thayer's Greek-English Lexicon adds to the evidence, that the word βαπτιζω (Baptizo) means (1) "To dip repeatedly, to immerge, submerge" (of vessels sunk), and (2) "To cleanse by dipping or submerging, to wash, to make clean with water; in the mid. and I aor. pass. to wash one's self, to bathe." So used in Mark Chapter 7 verse 4, and Luke Chapter 11, verse 38. [30]

---

[24] Vine, W. E., **Expository Dictionary of New Testament Words**, p.96,97

[25] *Ibid,* p.96,97

[26] Arndt & Gingrich, **A Greek-English Lexicon of the N.T.**, p.131

[27] Strong, James, **Exhaustive Concordance**, Greek Dictionary, 907

[28] Kittel, Gerhard, **Theological Dictionary of the New Testament**, p.545

[29] Liddell, Henry George & Scott, Robert, **A Greek-English Lexicon**, p.305

[30] Thayer, Joseph Henry, D. D., **Thayer's Greek-English Lexicon**, p.94

In the New Testament, Thayer explains, that Baptism is used particularly of the rite of sacred ablution, first instituted by John the Baptist, afterwards by Christ's command, received by the Christians and adjusted to the contents and nature of their religion. On βαπτισμα , it speaks of immersion in water, performed as a sign of the removal of sin, and administered to those, who impelled by a desire for salvation, sought admission to the benefits of Messiah's Kingdom. [31]

Trench is called in as another testimony to the fact that the word 'Baptizo' means "immersion, to plunge under or beneath". [32]

Thus Baptism means **"immersion, submersion,** and **emergence"**, or, "to dip" and is significant of the dyeing of a garment. This allows no place for Baptism to be by sprinkling. The Greek word used for sprinkling is ραντισμος (rantismos) and is a totally different word from that which speaks of Baptism. This word is used for sprinkling of blood, in Hebrews Chapter 12, and verse 24; 1 Peter Chapter 1, verse 2, and speaks of that cleansing through the blood of Jesus. [33]

In summary of this Section, we conclude that both Classical and Koine Greek usage of the word 'Baptizo', or 'Bapto' have the same connotation. Baptism is by immersion.

---

[31] *Ibid,* p.94

[32] Trench, Richard Chenevit, D. D., **Synonyms of the N. T.**, Associated Publishers & Authors Inc., Grand Rapids, Michigan, p.345

[33] Young, Robert, LL.D., **Analytical Concordance,** Greek Dictionary p.929. United Society for Christian Literature, Lutterworth Press, London, 1953, p.929

CHAPTER 3:

HISTORICAL PRACTICE
THE EARLY CHURCH

There are over one hundred references to Baptism in the New Testament, whether speaking of Ceremonial Washings, John's Baptism, or Christian Baptism.

The accounts given in the Gospels and the Acts show the absolute importance and significance of Baptism in the Early Church, and the emphasis placed upon it gives it a place in the foundational principles of the Doctrine of Christ. [34]

The record of these accounts of Baptism will be considered under their appropriate headings. Sufficient for the present comment is to see that the Early Church counted Water Baptism a vital ordinance in membership.

The converts on the Day of Pentecost were baptized immediately upon repentance. [35] The Samaritan believers were baptized immediately under the ministry of Philip the Evangelist. [36] Philip also baptized the Ethiopian upon confession of faith in Christ. [37] Saul was baptized straight away after Ananias came and healed him in response to the vision of the Lord. [38] Under the sovereign outpouring of the Spirit upon the Gentiles in the house of Cornelius, Peter recognized the fact that the Gentiles should be baptized in water, and thus he commanded it to be so. [39] Paul ministered Water Baptism immediately to converts in the various Gentile cities when they received the Gospel of Christ. This is seen in Philippi, and Corinth, as also other cities. [40]

In Ephesus Paul baptized those who had only received the

---

[34] Thompson, Hebrews 6:1-2
[35] Thompson, Acts 2:36-41
[36] *Ibid*, Acts 8:12-16
[37] *Ibid*, Acts 8:36-38
[38] *Ibid*, Acts 9:18
[39] *Ibid*, Acts 10:47-48
[40] *Ibid*, Acts 16:15,31-34; 18:8

Baptism of John. [41] And again, in several of the Church Epistles there are references and reminders to the saints of that which took place at their Baptism. [42]

It is impossible to read the New Testament without a recognition of the fact that the Early Church under Apostolic times placed very great importance and significance upon Baptism by immersion.

THE CHURCH FATHERS

The Church Fathers abound with references to the ordinance of Baptism. Even though the ordinance had become mixed with additions, corruptions, superstitions, and magic, nevertheless the Writings do show how important Baptism was in later Centuries.

HERMAS (A.D.100-140) said that Baptism was the very foundation of the Church, which is "builded upon the waters". JUSTIN declared that Baptism effected "regeneration" and "illumination". In the time of Hermas and Justin, the general view was that Baptism washed away all previous sins. ORIGEN and CYPRIAN both favoured Infant Baptism, claiming it was Apostolic custom. The first mention made of Infant Baptism, and that, an obscure one, was not until A.D.185, and this was IRENAEUS. [43]

We give several brief quotations from the Church Fathers as to the general attitude to Baptism.

A Letter of Clement says: "And now may the all-seeing God and Master 'of spirits' and Lord of 'all flesh' who chose the Lord Jesus Christ and us through Him 'to be His own people', grant every soul over whom His magnificent and holy Name has been invoked (a reference to the invocation of the Triune Name of God in Baptism), faith, fear, peace, patience, longsufferung, self-control, purity and sobriety." [44]

---

[41] Thompson, Acts 19:3-6

[42] *Ibid*, Romans 6:3-5; Galatians 3:27; Colossians 2:12

[43] Walker, Williston, **A History of the Christian Church**, Charles Scribner's Sons, New York U.S.A., 1970. p.87

[44] The Library of Christian Classics, **Early Church Fathers**, Vol. I. The Westminister Press, Philadelphia, U.S.A. p.73

From the Didache, or the Teaching of the Twelve Apostles, we quote: "Now about Baptism: this is how to baptize. Give public instruction of all these points, and then 'baptize' in running water, 'in the Name of the Father, and of the Son and of the Holy Spirit.' " [45] Also from the same source: "You must not let anyone eat or drink of your Eucharist except those who have been baptized in the Lord's Name." [46]

It shows that Baptism in the Name of the Father, and of the Son and of the Holy Spirit, or, Baptism in the Name of the Lord, was something generally known.

Bainton gives a sample of a 'Baptismal Service' after this had been corrupted by various traditions, and he tells of the candidate being immersed three times. He writes: "At the hour set for the Baptism the Bishop shall give thanks over oil and put it into a vessel; this is called the 'oil of thanksgiving'. And he shall take the other oil and excorcise it: this is called 'the oil of excorcism'. Then after the anointing by the Presbyter, taking hold of each of those about to be baptized, he commands them to renounce Satan, and all his servants and all his evil works. As they continue they go down into the water, and he who is baptizing puts his hand on the candidate saying:

Dost thou believe in God, the Father Almighty?

And he who is being baptized shall say: I believe.

Then taking his hand and placing it on his head, he shall baptize him once.

And then he shall say: Doest thou believe in Christ Jesus, the Son of God, who was born of the Holy Ghost of the Virgin Mary, and was crucified under Pontius Pilate, and was dead and buried, and rose again the third day, alive from the dead, and ascended into heaven, and sat at the right hand of the Father, and will come to judge the quick and the dead?

And when he says: I believe, he is baptized again.

---

[45] The Didache, **The Teaching of the Twelve Apostles,** The Library of Christian Classics, Early Church Fathers, The Westminister Press, Philadelphia, U.S.A. p.174

[46] *Ibid,* p.175

And again he shall say: Doest thou believe in (the) Holy Ghost, and the holy church, and the resurrection of the flesh?

He who is being baptized shall say accordingly: I believe, and so he is baptized a third time. [47]

Thus we see that Baptism was vital to the life of the Church, and this is attested to by Early Church history as in Apostolic times, and then in the later Centuries under the Church Fathers.

---

[47] Bainton, Roland H. **Early Christianity**, D. Van Nostrand Co. Inc., Princeton, New Jersey, U.S.A. 1960. p.138-139

CHAPTER 4:

MODERN THEOLOGICAL TENETS CONCERNING BAPTISM

Tracing from Early Church History through the Centuries under the Church Fathers up to Modern Times, we find much divergence and conflict over the meaning and place of Baptism in the Church.

The problem arises out of two main over-emphasis as pertaining to, what is spoken of as, the Sacrament of Baptism. Because of the implications of the word 'Sacrament' as pertaining to Romanism, the word 'Ordinance' will be used as being more suitable.

These two tendencies to extremes have been defined by T. C. Hammond as follows:

FIRST:

Over-evaluation. The Medieval Church over-evaluated this Ordinance until it became a corruption of 'mysteries of religion', rites, etc., always surrounded by spurious superstition, magic and mysticism.

SECONDLY:

Under-evaluation. Others under-valued the Ordinance saying that these were only external signs and that the grace that was attached to them was derived solely from the spiritual concepts in the minds of those who partook of the Sacraments. [48]

The Modern Theological Tenets possibly fall into four main groups as pertaining to Baptism. That is, (1) The non-Ordinance groups, such as the Salvation Army, the Quakers, and others who do not accept any form of Baptism; then (2) Roman Catholic, who believe that our original sin is dealt with in Baptism, resulting in justification. This teaches automatic grace is conferred in Baptism. Also (3) we have the Protestants, generally following the view of the Reformers, who place the emphasis on right reception and accompanying faith in and with Baptism; and (4) the Baptists, who confine Baptism to the ones who qualify by repentance and faith, or, regeneration. [49]

---

[48] Hammond, T. C., **In Understanding be Men,** Hazell Watson & Viney Ltd., Aylesbury, Bucks, Great Britain, 1971. p.169,170.

[49] *Ibid*, p.172,173.

Some Protestant groups hold Infant Baptism as fulfilling the Old Testament rite of circumcision.

Unger sums all up in two main classifications. Non-Baptists, or, Romanism, holding Baptismal Regeneration; and along with Romanism there is Greek Orthodox, most Lutheran Churches, many in the Church of England, and some Protestant Episcopal, all holding to the same doctrine or variations of it. Then the other classification is that of the Baptist Churches whose doctrine involves obligation, regeneration, faith and then Baptism by immersion. [50]

As the first and second main classifications will be briefly referred to in the following contents, we confine ourselves in the final part of this section to the group who do not accept or believe that the Ordinance of Baptism is necessary.

The Salvation Army, in their Doctrines set forth by William Booth clearly say: "As to The Salvation Army's firm conviction that these ceremonies are not necessary to salvation or essential to spiritual progress, this is why we do not observe them." [51]

While admitting that the Greek word 'Baptism' does mean immersion in water, they say that the use of the word is not confined to this meaning, concluding that "Water Baptism was evidently not intended to be perpetually observed." [52]

Booth continues: "Christ in the days of His flesh — being a Jew — observed certain Jewish Ordinances and customs, e.g., His Baptism by John, His going up to Jerusalem to the Feasts, and His celebration of the Passover; BUT NEITHER THIS, NOR THE FACT THAT CERTAIN CEREMONIES WERE OBSERVED BY THE EARLY CHRISTIANS, PROVES THAT WE ARE BOUND TO OBSERVE SUCH ORDINANCES NOW." (Capitals theirs) [53]

The Quakers statement of Faith is: "As there is one Lord and one

---

[50] Unger, Merrill F., Th.D. Ph.D., **Unger's Bible Dictionary,** Moody Press, Chicago, U.S.A. 1972. p.123.

[51] The Salvation Army, **Handbook of Doctrine,** International Headquarters, London, E.C., 4. 1940. p.168.

[52] *Ibid,* p.169.

[53] *Ibid,* p.169.

faith, so there is one Baptism; which is not the putting away the filth of the flesh, but the answer of a good conscience before God, by the resurrection of Jesus Christ. And this Baptism is a pure and spiritual thing, to wit, the Baptism of the Spirit and of fire, by which we are buried with Him, that being washed and purged from our sins, we may walk in newness of life; of which the Baptism of John was a figure which was commanded for a time and not to continue forever. As to the Baptism of infants, it is a mere human tradition, for which neither precept nor practice is to be found in all the Scripture." [54]

Rejection of Baptism by the Quakers is but a part of their rejection of the means of grace in general. For Water Baptism they substitute the "Baptism of the Spirit and fire." The Salvation Army takes a similar position. It puts Baptism in the same category with circumcision, clipping the hair, footwashing, and rejects Baptism together with these "abrogated Jewish ceremonies that were never intended to bind our consciences." [55]

BAPTISM AS A MEANS OF GRACE

Baptism, in most of the groups who baptize, is looked upon as a 'means of grace'. By 'means of grace' is meant all the ordinances of God whereby we receive His Covenantal blessings. Means through which God's activity towards us becomes known. It does not carry the thought of works by which we earn the grace of God. [56]

The Lutheran Doctrine (Lutheranism in America) states it this way: "Above all, we must clearly recognize and maintain that Baptism is a means of grace. Baptism is no more and no less than a Divinely ordained means whereby God in a special manner conveys and imparts to the person baptized the remission of sins provided for him by Christ's sacrifice. Baptism is not a work that we offer to God, but

---

[54] Bettenson, Henry, **Documents of the Christian Church,** Oxford University Press, New York, U.S.A. 1954. p.358.

[55] Pieper, Francis, **Christian Dogmatics,** Concordia Publishing House, Saint Louis, Mo., U.S.A. 1953. p.253.

[56] Hammond, T. C., **In Understanding be Men,** Hazell Watson & Viney Ltd., Aylesbury, Bucks, Great Britain, 1971. p.169.

one that God does to us and by which God offers and presents the remission of sins." [57]

Pieper teaches that Baptism is a means of imparting the remission of sins, basing his remarks upon Acts Chapter 2 and verse 38, where Peter calls on the multitude to be baptized in the Name of Jesus Christ 'for the remission of sins'. Also he quotes Acts Chapter 22 and verse 16 where Ananias calls on Paul (Saul) to 'wash away his sins'. Pieper goes on to tell that through Baptism and the remission of sins, the Word of God calls forth faith, or strengthens it, and is a means of regeneration and renewing of the Holy Ghost, as Paul wrote to Titus. [58]

The teaching of Romanism is that Baptism imparts grace even though the baptized person does not have faith, that there the hand of one lays hold of the forgiveness of sins offered in Baptism. [59]

A. BAPTISMAL REGENERATION

With regards to the Doctrine of Baptismal Regeneration, we note briefly its content.

Baptismal Regeneration teaches that the New Birth or Regeneration is the direct result of Water Baptism. The teaching is based upon the words of Christ in the Gospel of Mark, Chapter 16 and verse 16, where Jesus said: "He that believeth and is baptized shall be saved, and he that believeth not shall be damned." It is claimed by those who adhere to this Doctrine that there can be no salvation apart from Water Baptism. This Scripture is combined with John's Gospel, chapter 3 and verse 5, where Jesus told Nicodemus that a man must "be born of water and of the Spirit" in order to see or enter the Kingdom of God; and that the 'water' spoken of here refers to Water Baptism.

Further, it is contended that Water Baptism is the place where a person's sins are washed away, after calling on the Name of the Lord through the Trinitarian Formula of Matthew Chapter 28, verse 19, and

---

[57] Pieper, Francis D. D., **Christian Dogmatics,** Concordia Publishing House, Saint Louis, Missouri, U.S.A. 1953. p.263.

[58] *Ibid,* p.264.

[59] *Ibid,* p.265.

according to Acts Chapter 22 and verse 16, where Ananias said to Paul: "Arise and be baptized, and **wash** away thy sins, calling on the Name of the Lord."

Then again, 1 Peter Chapter 3 and verse 21 is added as further proof of the doctrine, that "even Baptism doth also now save us." Thus Water Baptism is purported to be the means of Regeneration, of Remission of sins, and entrance into the Kingdom of God. All who are not water baptized are therefore damned.

However, in moving on from this area, it is worthy to note that the real emphasis in Mark's Gospel is not upon Baptism first, but on believing, and then Baptism. "He that BELIEVETH and is BAPTIZED shall be saved, but he that BELIEVETH NOT (and it does not add, 'and is **not** baptized') shall be damned."

This will be elaborated upon further in the section pertaining to the pre-requisites for Baptism in the New Testament.

Thomas Aquinas (A.D.1225-1274) defines the Doctrine of Baptismal Regeneration by saying: "By Baptism the recipient is regenerated, and original and previous personal sins are pardoned, though the tendency to sin is not obliterated. Man is now given the grace, if he will use it, to resist sin, and the lost power to attain to the Christian virtues." [60]

B. BAPTISMAL SANCTIFICATION

The teaching which can only be defined as 'Baptismal Sanctification may be summed up as follows.

Though the believer is born again and has entered into the Kingdom of God by New Birth, yet there remains inbred sin, the root of sin, though his sins have been forgiven. In order for this root of sin to be cleansed out of the person, or to be eradicated, obedience in Water Baptism is that means of grace whereby this is effected. In Water Baptism the 'old man', the old life with its inbred desires to sin is destroyed; it is 'putoff', so that the believer is now 'wholly sanctified' by the Waters of Baptism.

---

[60] Walker, Williston, **A History of the Christian Church,** Charles Scribner's Sons, New York, U.S.A. 1970. p.247.

Baptismal Sanctification is thus aligned with a 'second work of grace', whereby the 'old nature', the 'sin-nature' is eradicated. All of this is based upon the teachings of the Apostle Paul where he reminds the baptized that they were indeed buried with Christ in Baptism, and have 'put off the old man with his deeds' and that 'the body of sin' has been destroyed. [61]

However, Scripture, as well as experience of every living believer, proves that there is certainly an over-emphasis and great misunderstanding of the Scriptures which speak of these things. This Doctrine is closely associated with the Doctrine of 'Sinless Perfection' or 'Eradication', except that here the means of grace is Water Baptism.

C. INFANT BAPTISM

As far as can be gathered, Infant Baptism is not mentioned in Apostolic times; the first mention of it being about A.D. 185, by one of the Church Fathers named Irenaeus. [62] Infant Baptism was absorbed into the rites of the Church of the Middle Ages with all of its surrounding innovations.

The teachings on Infant Baptism fall possibly into two main streams; one stream holding that in Infant Baptism, the child is saved, or else has a guarantee of salvation. The other holding that the child is not saved or regenerated but it is brought into Covenant relationship with God through the parents, with the possibility of being saved.

The Anabaptists, as they were nicknamed (or re-baptizers) were those who denied the reality of their Infant Baptism, and were then baptized again upon their repentance and faith, or, after knowing as in definite experience with Christ, the regenerating work of the Holy Spirit. [63]

Luther says concerning Infant Baptism, that it has been "practiced since the beginning of the Church" and it comes to us "from the Apostles and has been preserved ever since their time." He freely

---

[61] Thompson, Romans 6:1-6, p.164.

[62] Walker, Williston, **A History of the Christian Church,** Charles Scribner's Sons, New York, U.S.A. 1970. p.87.

[63] Walker, Williston, **A History of the Christian Church,** p.326.

admits, however, that Infant Baptism, is neither explicitly commanded or mentioned in Scripture. There are no "specific passages" referring to Infant Baptism. [64]

Althaus, in defining the teaching of Luther on Baptism, continues to write, that "Baptizing with water is, at first glance, a human act. Men do not, however, baptize in their own name but in God's Name. And men have not invented nor discovered Baptism; rather it is instituted and commanded by God Himself, and it is God Himself Who acts in it. To be baptized in God's Name is to be baptized not by men but by God Himself ... It is water used according to God's command and connected with God's Word." [65]

It is evident that the Doctrine of Baptismal Regeneration flavours the whole thing.

Luther places Baptism in the very center of the Christian life. His understanding of Baptism exactly expresses his Doctrine of Justification. [66]

What does Luther declare?

> "Baptism conveys all of salvation. It effects forgivenness of sins, delivers from death and the devil, and grants eternal salvation to all that believe. Through Baptism I am promised that I shall be saved and have eternal life, both in body and soul. Baptism does not give a particular grace, not only a part of salvation, but simply the entire grace of God, the entire Christ and the Holy Spirit with His gifts." [67]

Presbyterianism puts it this way:

> "Not only those that do actually profess faith and obedience unto Christ, but also infants of one or both of the believing parents, are to be baptized ... grace and salvation are not so inseparably annexed to it, as that ... all that are baptized are undoubtedly regenerated ..." [68]

---

[64] Althaus, Paul, **The Theology of Martin Luther,** Fortress Press, Philadelphia, U.S.A. 1966. p.359,361.

[65] *Ibid,* p.353.

[66] *Ibid,* p.356.

[67] Althaus, Paul, **The Theology of Martin Luther,** p.353.

[68] Bettenson, Henry, **Documents of the Christian Church,** Oxford University Press, New York, U.S.A. 1954. p.351.

Methodism also records:

> "Baptism is a visible admission of children into the congregation of Christ's flock, and the rite may be administered either by sprinkling, pouring, or immersion. Though the word 'Infant Baptism' is not found in Scripture yet the thing signified is . . . In adult Baptism there is a seal of a conversion accomplished; in Infant Baptism, it is a prophecy of conversion to come (Banks). And the prophecy is to be accomplished through instruction, example and counsel (Banks)." [69]

The Doctrine of Infant Baptism is founded upon an interpretation of the Scriptures which speak of those being baptized and 'their house' when they believed on the Lord Jesus Christ. It is spoken of as 'Household Baptism', assuming that children were present at the time. The Scriptures mention whole families being baptized, as can be seen in 1 Corinthians Chapter 1 and verses 14 through 16; and also Acts Chapter 16, verses 15,33. And then again, the children were brought to Jesus and He blessed them with the blessings of the Kingdom of God, as Mark Chapter 10, verses 13 through 16 speak. It is thus proposed that children may therefore be baptized and receive the benefits of the Kingdom.

One final prominent analogy is that of Circumcision as performed under the Old Covenant whereby children were brought into the blessings and privileges of the Abrahamic Covenant. Thus it is contended that, seeing Water Baptism is the New Testament Circumcision, then what is there to forbid children receiving the New Covenant blessings through this Ordinance? [70] Jesus Himself said: "Suffer the little children to come unto Me, and forbid them not, for of such is the Kingdom of Heaven." [71]

In bringing this section to a close, we see that the above groups follow Infant Baptism with the basic thought of salvation through Baptism, and is closely linked with Baptismal Regeneration. The other

---

[69] Oliver, Samuel, **Synopsis of Christian Theology,** The Epworth Press, 25-35 City Road, E.C.I., London.

[70] Pieper, Francis, **Christian Dogmatics,** Concordia Publishing House, Saint Louis, Missouri, U.S.A. 1953. p.277.

[71] Thompson, Matthew 19:14, p.23 N.T.

area is seen in the following teaching, which teaches Infant Baptism but does not hold to Baptismal Regeneration. This grouping believes that Baptism commits the parents of the believing with the children to salvation.

J. Robinson Gregory defines it by describing the effect of Baptism upon a child. "Baptism plainly cannot effect or secure what has already been effected and secured for every human being by the Second Adam. He shows clearly that Baptism is not a cancelling of entailed sentence of condemnation for sin of the First Adam, as this is done by Christ. Also, Baptism does not impart to the child a capacity for restraining, renewing, or sanctifying action of the Holy Spirit. Nor does it impart reason and conscience, for all children are born with such. Baptism does not put away the guilt of personal sin, nor does it effect personal adoption into the family of God, which can only be by faith in Christ, which faith only comes by hearing and hearing by the Word of God. Neither does Baptism effect purification of the heart, which comes through obedience only." [72]

In conclusion, Gregory says that "Baptism was not invented by the Lord or by the Apostles. The Jews baptized proselytes, and thus we see Baptism following through into the New Testament Church. There we see Households being baptized. The **principle** of Infant Baptism is plainly acknowledged. To prevent Infant Baptism would have required a command forbidding it. The burden of proof therefore lies upon those who deny, not upon those who affirm. Circumcision, which was the Seal of the Old Covenant was administered to infants; thus the Jew would naturally treat the Seal of the New Covenant in the same manner." [73] He summarizes it all by: "Baptism of an adult is his formal profession of faith. Baptism of infants commits both the parents and the Church to the training of the one who is thus made a disciple." [74]

---

[72] Gregory, J. R., **The Theological Student,** 25-35 City Road, E. C. London, 1910. p.230,231.

[73] Gregory, J. R., **The Theological Student,** p.228,229.

[74] *Ibid,* p.232.

D. A CLEAR CONSCIENCE

The Apostle Peter, writing to the strangers scattered abroad, when referring to Baptism tells them: "The like figure whereunto even Baptism doth now **save us** (not the putting away of the filth of the flesh, but **the answer of a good conscience** toward God), by the resurrection of Jesus Christ. . ." [75]

Peter clearly admits that it is not merely the washing away of the filth of the flesh, as in the taking of a bath to cleanse the body, or having the body washed with pure water (Hebrews 10:22), that saves us, but it is the answer of a good conscience towards God. This is the thing that matters.

Deducted from this Scripture has come various conclusions. Some persons claiming that it does not matter whether a person is sprinkled, poured upon, immersed, or whether they are even baptized at all; the only mattering before God is to have a clear conscience.

Others, in line with this above, relative to the words of a Formula, state that the words of a Formula do not matter. It matters not if Matthew Chapter 28 and verse 19 is quoted, as the command of Jesus; or whether the Name of the Lord Jesus Christ, as in the Book of Acts, is invoked; or, whether any words are spoken at all. It is claimed that the only thing that matters before God is the condition of the heart, "the answer of a good conscience toward God." God does not really concern Himself with the Mode or the Formula, so long as a person has a clear conscience.

Pieper, in his book, comments: "Baptism is not a matter of choice, but a Divine Ordinance; still one may not assert an absolute necessity of Baptism or say that no one can obtain remission of sins and be saved without Baptism." [76]

However, the whole point of the matter here is this. Conscience is not the final court of appeal before God. The believer must have his conscience subject to the Word of God which alone is the final and infallible court of appeal. Paul could say that "my conscience also

---

[75] Thompson, 1 Peter 3:21. p.244. N.T.

[76] Pieper, Francis, **Christian Dogmatics,** p.280.

bearing me witness in the Holy Ghost." [77]

The Holy Spirit has inspired the Word of God and our consciences must line up with that Word. Only then can the believer have the answer of a good conscience towards God. If the Word of God has prescribed Baptism as to its Mode, and if it has declared a proper significance and interpretation of Baptism, then every believer will only have a clear conscience before God as the Word is obeyed in true faith.

BAPTISM FOR THE DEAD

The Latter Day Saints hold the Doctrine of "Baptism for the dead." This teaching and practice is based upon an interpretation of a passage of Scripture found in the Epistle to the Corinthians. Paul, in writing about the resurrection, refers to a custom which was then in vogue in Corinth. In proving a point concerning the resurrection, he brings in this custom to show that even others outside of the Church of Corinth had a doctrine which showed belief in the resurrection.

He writes: "Else what shall they do which are baptized for the dead, if the dead rise not at all? why are they then baptized for the dead?" [78]

It is upon this lone Scripture that the custom of "Baptizing for the dead" is founded. Thayer comments: 'On behalf of the dead, i.e., to promote their eternal salvation by undergoing baptism in their stead.' [79]

Kittel, in reference to this passage advances: "There is no contradiction in 1 Corinthians Chapter 15, and verse 29, as Paul sees it, even though this refers to a groping attempt, unconditionally accepted by him, to apply salvation in Christ to the unbaptized dead. It is more likely, however, that the argument is purely tactical; Paul is referring ironically to the inconsistency of the Corinthians. Indeed, he may even be alluding to a non-Christian practice of the Mysteries. Many Gnostic sects are reported to have held vicarious baptisms. It is

---

[77] Thompson, Romans 9:1. p.167. N.T.

[78] Thompson, 1 Corinthians 15:29. p.186. N.T.

[79] Thayer, Joseph Henry, D. D., **Thayer's Greek-English Lexicon**, p.94.

thus legitimate to seek a pagan origin." [80]

In Unger's Bible Dictionary is listed three suggested interpretations as to what Paul meant in this reference. These are (1) that heretics had a custom, supposed to be referred to by the Apostle Paul, by which persons who had been already baptized were baptized again for the benefit of those who had died unbaptized but believing; hence "for the benefit of the dead." Then (2), others say it refers to the confession of the baptized, when they confessed "I believe in the resurrection of the dead." This being a confession of faith that the dead should rise. Then, (3) others speak for the martyrs who had died, and this 'in behalf' was for them and their testimony, that all would be raised together. [81]

In concluding this portion, we would add this explanation. Paul in no way sanctions this custom with Divine authority. It will be noticed that Paul says "**they**" and not "**we**", [82] as he does generally in other references to Baptism. It is a third class outside of the Apostles and outside the Corinthian saints. Heathen religions have their 'Baptismal Waters' for salvation, purifications of the soul, and other cleansings, but Baptism is only for the repentant and the believing ones who have been regenerated by the Holy Spirit. There is no chance beyond death, and none can be baptized in behalf of the dead before God. If the dead did not repent and believe while they were alive in this world, then it is in vain for any one to submit to baptism for them after they have died. Salvation is only in this life, and that for the repentant and believing. Life eternal will be granted only on this basis.

---

[80] Kittel, Gerhard, **Theological Dictionary of the New Tesament,** p.542.

[81] Unger, Merrill F. **Unger's Bible Dictionary,** Moody Press, Chicago, U.S.A. 1972.

[82] Thompson, 1 Corinthians 15:29. p.186. N.T.

CHAPTER 5:

WATER BAPTISM IN THE GOSPELS

CEREMONIAL WASHINGS OF THE LAW

Jewry, as a nation, was already familiar with the "Doctrine of Baptisms" by that which was set forth in the ceremonial washings of the Law. [83]

The Greek word for 'Baptisms' used in Hebrews Chapter 6 and verse 2 is βαπτισμων , as seen earlier, and means "washings". The same word is used again in Hebrews Chapter 9 and verse 10, where βαπτισμοις is translated "divers washings."

In his Exposition of Hebrews, Pink comments on these verses, saying:

> "Of the doctrine of Baptisms, verse 2. Had the translators understood the scope and meaning of this passage it is more doubtful if they had given the rendering they did to this particular clause.
>
> It will be observed that the word 'baptize' is in the plural number, and if Scripture be allowed to interpret Scripture there will be no difficulty in ascertaining what is here referred to.
>
> It is neither Christian Baptism (Mt 28:10), the Baptism of the Spirit (Acts 1:5), nor the Baptism of suffering (Mt 20:23), which is here in view, but the carnal ablutions which obtained under the Mosaic economy.
>
> The Greek word is 'baptismos'. It is found four times on the pages of the N.T., in Mark 7:4,5 and Heb. 6:2, 9:10. In each of the other three instances the word is rendered 'washings'.
>
> In Mark 7 it is the 'washing of cups and pans.' In Heb. 9:10, it is 'meats and drinks and divers washings and carnal (fleshly) ordinances,' concerning which it is said, they were 'imposed until the time of reformation'."[84]

Further to this, Pink writes:

> "It is to be noted that our verse speaks of 'The Doctrine of Baptisms.'

---

[83] Thompson, Hebrews 6:2. p.230 N.T.

[84] Pink, Arthur W. **An Exposition of Hebrews,** Baker Book House, Grand Rapids, Michigan, U.S.A. 1971. p.280.

There was a definite teaching connected with the ceremonial ablutions of Judaism. They were designed to impress upon the Israelites that Jehovah was a holy God, and that none who were defiled could enter into His presence.

These references in Heb 6:1 and 9:10 look back to the 'washings' denoted in passages as Ex 30:18,19, Lev 16:4; Num 19:19, etc. Typically these 'washings' noted that all the defiling effects of sin must be removed ere the worshipper could approach unto the Lord.

They foreshadowed that perfect and eternal cleansing from sin which the atoning blood of Christ was to provide for His people. They had no intrinsic efficacy in themselves; they were but figures, hence, we are told they sanctified only 'to the purifying of the flesh' (Heb 9:13). Those 'washings' effected nought but an external and ceremonial purification; they 'could not make him that did the service perfect as pertaining to the conscience' (Heb 9:9)."[85]

The Old Covenant ceremonials or divers washings in water simply shadowed forth Water Baptism in its outward and inward significance. It prepared Jewry for the New Testament Baptism which would be 'into Christ'.

We briefly refer to several of these Old Testament "Baptisms" or ceremonial washings, which pointed to New Testament Baptism.

(1) Aaron and his sons as Priests were washed in water; that is, they were wholly bathed in water in their consecration to the Priest-hood. [86] (2) The leper, as part of his ceremonial cleansings, had to be wholly bathed or washed in water before coming into the Congregation of the Camp of the Lord. [87] (3) In the purification from uncleannesses, the 'Waters of Separation' played a vital part. All persons involved, whether clean or unclean, had to wash in water in order to remain in the Camp of the Lord. [88]

All of these things were "divers washings", and they taught the Doctrine of Baptisms under the Old Covenant thus preparing the way

---

[85] Pink, Arthur W. **An Exposition of Hebrews,** Baker Book House, Grand Rapids, Michigan, U.S.A. 1971. p.280,281.

[86] Thompson Chain Reference Bible, Exodus 29:4; Leviticus 8:6.

[87] *Ibid,* Leviticus 13:8,9.

[88] *Ibid,* Numbers Ch.19.

for New Covenant Baptism with Christ.

The Apostle Paul even takes the historical record of Israel as a nation passing through the Red Sea and the Cloud as being a type of Baptism of the nation 'in water' and 'in the Spirit'. [89] As Israel was baptized unto (lit. 'into') Moses, the Mediator of the Old Covenant, so the believer is baptized into Christ, the Mediator of the New Covenant. By all of these things above, the Hebrew mind was prepared, and thus these "divers washings" became a 'School-master to bring them to Christ'.

It is to be noticed also that even in the time of John's ministry, the Jewish rulers had a form of Baptism which brought Gentile proselytes into Covenant relationship with the God of Israel.

We quote from Myer Pearlman who gives an illustration of this fact. Pearlman writes:

> "The word 'baptize' in the formula means literally 'to dip' or 'to immerse'. This interpretation is confirmed by Greek scholars and Church Historians; even scholars belonging to Churches which baptize by sprinkling admit that immersion was the earliest mode.
>
> Moreover, there is good reason for believing that to the Jews of Apostolic times the command to be 'baptized' would suggest immersion.
>
> They were acquainted with 'proselyte's Baptism' which signified a heathen's conversion to Judaism. The convert stood up to his neck in water while the Law was read to him, after which he plunged himself beneath the water as a sign that he was cleansed from the defilements of heathenism and had begun to live a new life as a member of God's Covenant people"[90]

This was all preparatory to the Baptism of John followed by Christian Baptism.

THE BAPTISM OF JOHN, OR JOHN'S BAPTISM

It was fitting for God at the close of the 400 'Silent Years' to send

---

[89] Thompson's Chain Reference Bible, 1 Corinthians 10:1-3, p.181, N.T.

[90] Pearlman, Myer, **Knowing the Doctrines of the Bible,** Gospel Publishing House, Springfield, Mo., U.S.A. 1945. p.353.

John the Baptist as the Forerunner of Messiah. "There was a man sent from God whose name was John." [91]

When John came on the scene of Judaism, religion had degenerated to a state of hypocritical fundamentalism, as seen in the Pharisees, on the one hand, and ceremonialism and formalism, as seen in the Temple ritual and the Priesthood. And again, legalism abounded as seen in the Scribes who were the interpreters of the Law, and opposite to this was radical Modernism as represented in the great unbelief of the Sadducees.

Though John was born of a Priestly line through his father, Zacharias, God sent him outside of the establishment of his day and John became, as Matthew records, "the voice of one crying in the wilderness." [92] And what a wilderness it was spiritually speaking. There was need of a voice, a voice of God, a voice from God and not merely an echo of other men's words and opinions.

The Word of God came to John in the wilderness commanding him to preach repentance, restitution and faith in the coming Messiah and His Kingdom, and this was to be attested to in Water Baptism. This was spoken of as 'John's Baptism' or 'The Baptism of John'. [93]

As John began to preach, saying: "Repent, for the Kingdom of Heaven is at hand", baptizing people unto repentance and faith, the Pharisees challenged John's authority to baptize. They themselves accepted proselytes into the Judaistic Faith by the rite of Baptism, but that was on the authority of the religious leaders. Where did John get his authority from for his Baptism? The ones sent to John were Levites and Priests sent by the Pharisees. They knew that "divers baptisms" in their implications pointed to that "washing" which Messiah was to bring. Hence they challenged John: "Why baptizeth thou then if thou be not the Christ, nor Elias, neither that prophet?" John humbly confessed that he was but 'A voice' crying in the wilderness; he confessed that his Water Baptism was a pointer to a greater Baptism which the Messiah Himself would bring, that being, the Baptism of the

---

[91] Thompson's Chain Reference Bible, John 1:6, p.96 N.T.
[92] *Ibid,* Matthew 3:3, p.4, N.T.
[93] *Ibid,* Acts 18:25; 19:3, p.147, N.T.

Holy Spirit. [94]

John's Baptism in water by immersion signified the need of and acceptance of repentance. Multitudes responded to this Baptism. The religious leaders, however, were too proud and self-righteous to accept it, yet they dare not speak out against it. It was humiliating for them to think that they had to be identified with that which brought common and unclean Gentiles into the Faith of Judaism. For this reason Jesus challenged them after they had questioned His authority: "The Baptism of John, was it from heaven or of men?" [95]

They dare not answer. They would not commit themselves. If they said it was of men, the people would repel them, as the people did count John to be a Prophet. If they said it was 'of heaven', then why did they not accept it, and submit themselves to it? They stood self-condemned. [96]

The Pharisees were plagued with continual ceremonial "washings", (Greek $\beta\alpha\pi\tau\iota\sigma\mu\omega\iota$), as seen in Mark Chapter 7 and verse 4, such as the washing of hands, of cups and plates, etc., yet inwardly they were corrupted and defiled. They needed the true "washing", the real, the inner and that spiritual Baptism to which John's Baptism pointed. Water Baptism is significant of a bath, a spiritual washing which takes place in regeneration.

The ceremonial and divers washings of the Law prophesied of the inner spiritual washing by water of the Word, primarily, and then pointed to Water Baptism, which witnessed the former.

John pointed to the true Baptism and cleansing by **water and blood** through Messiah's ministry. The spiritual significance is set out in Titus Chapter 3 and verse 5 in "**the washing of regeneration and renewing of the Holy Ghost**", and confirmed by John in Chapter 3 and verse 5, where a person must be "**born of water and of the Spirit**" to be able to see or enter the Kingdom of God.

Paul reminds the Corinthians that they had been "washed". [97]

---

[94] Thompson's Chain Reference Bible, John 1:19-33, p.96,97.

[95] *Ibid,* Matthew 21:25; Mark 11:30; Luke 20:4; p.25,51,88.

[96] *Ibid,* Luke 7:30, p.69.

[97] Thompson's Chain Reference Bible, 1 Corinthians 6:11, p.178.

Ananias had called on him to "wash away his sins" in Baptism. [98] The outer points to the inner, the literal to the spiritual.

BAPTISM BY CHRIST'S DISCIPLES

When John introduced Jesus as the Messiah to the Jewish nation, his own ministry began to fade into insignificance. John himself recognized that "I must decrease, He must increase." [99]

It is helpful to understand that the ultimate purpose of John's Baptism was to inaugurate the ministry of Messiah. Even though John was cousin to Jesus after the flesh, it seems evident that he did not fully know or realize that He was to be the Messiah. For this reason he was given an express word that the One who would be the Messiah would be manifested at a Water Baptismal service, and that John would recognize Him by seeing the Holy Spirit descending and remaining upon Him. [100]

As Jesus began to minister, the multitudes who had flocked to John the Forerunner, now flock to hear the Christ he pointed to. So great was the popularity of Jesus at this time that more disciples were baptized by Him than by John. [101]

The Scriptures, however, tell us "Jesus Himself baptized not, but His disciples.

The reason for this will be seen in the following section. Jesus Himself had not need to submit to John's Baptism, for it was a Baptism unto repentance, a Baptism for sinners accompanied by confession of sin. Jesus was baptized "to fulfill all righteousness." [102]

Unger brings out the thought concerning Jesus fulfilling all righteousness by referring back to the requirements of the Levitical Law. All priests were consecrated when they 'began to be about 30 years of age' (Num 4:3; Lke 3:23). This consecration was twofold. First the washing (baptism), and then the anointing (Ex 29:4-7; Lev 8:6-36).

---

[98] *Ibid,* Acts 22:16, p.152.
[99] *Ibid,* John 3:30, p.99.
[100] *Ibid,* John 3:34, 1:30-33, p.97,99.
[101] *Ibid,* John 4:1-2, p.99.
[102] Thompson's Chain Reference Bible, Matthew 3:15, p.5.

When John on Jordan's banks "washed" (baptized) Jesus, the heavens were opened and the Holy Spirit came upon Him. This was the Priestly anointing of Him Who was not only a Priest by Divine appointment, but an Eternal Priest (Psa 110:4), and Who was thus Divinely consecrated for the work of redemption (Mt 3:16; Acts 4:27; 10:38). [103]

Thus we concur that the Messiah confirmed the message of John the Baptist by being baptized of him, and then preaching repentance and faith, attested to by Water Baptism, all of which would be included in the New Covenant Church in due time, with fuller implications.

THE POST-RESURRECTION COMMAND OF CHRIST

In Matthew's Gospel, Chapter 28 verse 19, is given, what is spoken of as, 'The Great Commission'. To quote it in full, Jesus said: "Go ye therefore, and teach (disciple) all nations, baptizing them in the name of the Father, and of the Son, and of the Holy Ghost: Teaching them to observe all things whatsoever I have commanded you: and, lo, I am with you alway, even unto the end of the world. Amen."

In Mark's Gospel the account reads: "He that believeth and is baptized shall be saved, and he that believeth not shall be damned." [104] Only Matthew and Mark make any specific reference to Water Baptism in their account of the Commission of Jesus to His disciples just prior to His ascension.

The question that presents itself here is this. Why did Jesus command the disciples to go into all the world, and baptize in the name of the Father, and of the Son, and of the Holy Spirit when the Baptism of John was already in operation and had been ordained of God Himself? Why was this commandment given? Was not John's Baptism sufficient and suitable for the Church and all nations? Was there something lacking in John's Baptism?

The answer is partly seen in the following comments. John's Baptism, as indeed his whole ministry, was simply a pointer to the

---

[103] Unger, Merrill F., Th.D. Ph.D., **Unger's Bible Dictionary**, Moody Press, Chicago, U.S.A. 1972. p.122.

[104] Thompson's Chain Reference, Mark 16:16, p.58.

Messiah and His ministry. John stands at the close of the Old Covenant Dispensation and points to Jesus who stands at the opening of the New Covenant Dispensation. The true inner and spiritual cleansing from sin, shadowed forth in John's Baptism was only to be found in Messiah Himself. This spiritual 'washing' would be made available for all who repented and believed in Messiah's work of redemption.

Under John's ministry, ceremonial cleansings by animal blood and divers washings in water were still carried on in Judaism. When Christ Jesus died on the cross and "blood and water" flowed from His side, [105] it brought a cessation forever to the Old Testament ceremonials. This was the true 'washing'; to be washed in the blood and water which poured forth from the wounded side of Jesus. He was the fulfilment of all types. These were fulfilled and abolished in His sinless perfect once-for-all sacrifice for sin.

When Christ Jesus gave the command, His DEATH, BURIAL and RESURRECTION had been accomplished. The finished work of redemption had been manifest. He was about to ascend to the Father's Right Hand of power and be given the exalted Name of the Lord Jesus Christ. [106]

Hence the moment Jesus gave the Baptismal Command as written in Matthew's Gospel, it nullified John's Baptism.

It will be found in due time that John's Baptism, though truly ordained of God, was temporary and transitional. John's Baptism became inadequate and incomplete for the New Testament Church.

The reasons for these above conclusions will be explained more fully in the closing section of this thesis, before the summary and conclusion. The main thing to be remembered here is the fact that Christian Baptism in the Name of the Eternal Godhead cancelled out John's Baptism, after the Death, Burial and Resurrection of Jesus Christ, the Son of God.

---

[105] *Ibid,* John 19:34,35, p.121.
[106] Thompson's Chain Reference Bible, Acts 2:31-36, p.126.

CHAPTER 6:

WATER BAPTISM IN THE BOOK OF ACTS

PRE-REQUISITES TO WATER BAPTISM

Before taking a look at the records of Baptism in the Book of Acts, it will be profitable to consider the pre-requisites to Water Baptism, that is, Christian Baptism.

We consider these in their proper order:

1. **Repentance:**

   The first pre-requisite is repentance. Jesus said that repentance and remission of sins should be preached in His Name among all nations. [107]

   Peter confirmed this in his Sermon at Pentecost to the multitude who gathered at Jerusalem for the Feast. He said to them: "Repent and be baptized every one of you . . ." [108]

   The writer of Hebrews lists 'repentance from dead works' as the First Principle of the Doctrine of Christ. [109]

   It is worthy to note that 'Repent' was the first word of John's message (Mt 3:2), the first word of Messiah's message (Mt 4:17), as well as being the first word of Peter's message at Pentecost (Acts 2:38). It was also the first word in Paul's preaching (Acts 20:21).

   Thus repentance — a change of mind towards God and sin, a right about turn — preceded Water Baptism. This is the very first pre-requisite.

2. **Faith towards God through Christ:**

   The next pre-requisite to Water Baptism is faith towards God through Jesus Christ. Jesus emphasized this word in Mark's Gospel-Commission.

---

[107] Thompson's Chain Reference Bible, Luke 24:47, p.96
[108] *Ibid*, Acts 2:38, p.126
[109] *Ibid*, Hebrews 6:1-2, p.230

"He that believeth and is baptized shall be saved, and he that believeth not shall be damned." [110]

The account of Philip's ministry in Samaria tells us: "When they believed Philip preaching the things concerning the Kingdom of God, and the Name of Jesus Christ, they were baptized, both men and women." [111]

As Philip preached Jesus to the Ethiopian, they came to water and the Ethiopian asked Philip if there was anything that hindered him from being baptized. Philip said: "If thou believest with all thine heart, thou mayest. And he answered and said, I believe that Jesus Christ is the Son of God." [112] Then Philip baptized him.

The first word of the Gospel is 'Repent', and the second word is 'Believe'. [113] Faith or believing is that whole trust in God for the saving work of salvation and cleansing from sin. It is not a mental acceptance of historical facts concerning the person of Jesus. The Philippian jailor was baptized after he believed in the Lord Jesus Christ, after he believed in God. [114] The Corinthians first believed and then were baptized under Paul's ministry. [115] Even John's Baptism involved both repentance and faith. [116]

Genuine repentance precedes saving faith. It is impossible to have saving faith apart from it. For these reasons, Baptism for the dead, and Infant Baptism, are repudiated. The Waters of Baptism as a process of regeneration become redundant also. The one who is baptized must be a repentant and believing person first. These are the two dominant pre-requisites to Water Baptism as seen in the Gospels and the Acts. They have never been abrogated. It is truly 'believer's Baptism'. Thus repentance, faith, then Baptism. This is Divine order.

---

[110] Thompson's Chain Reference Bible, Mark 16:16, p.58
[111] *Ibid*, Acts 8:12,13, p.133
[112] *Ibid*, Acts 8:36,37, p.134
[113] *Ibid*, Mark 1:15, p.37
[114] *Ibid*, Acts 16:31-34
[115] *Ibid*, Acts 18:8, p.146
[116] *Ibid*, Acts 19:4, p.147

WATER BAPTISM RECORDS IN THE ACTS

A. IN JERUSALEM

The first reference and record of Water Baptism in the Book of Acts is found in the chapter of events which took place on the Day of Pentecost, Acts Chapter 2.

It cannot be over-emphasized that which took place here is that which pertains to the birth of the New Testament Church.

The disciples numbered about 120 and as they continued in one place of one accord unto the Day of Pentecost, the Feast of the fiftieth day, the Scripture tells us that the Holy Spirit descended suddenly from heaven as a mighty rushing wind, filling the house where they were sitting. Cloven tongues like as of fire appeared and sat upon the head of each of the disciples, both men and women. All were filled with the Spirit, speaking in other tongues as the Spirit gave them utterance.

As the multitude gathered together, Jews out of every nation under heaven, they were made to realize that the supernatural manifestations seen and heard were evidences of the risen and exalted Lord. He had received the Promise of the Father and had poured forth this upon the waiting disciples.

The speaking in tongues ceased as Peter stood with the eleven other Apostles and began to preach the first 'Pentecostal Sermon'. This Sermon lays down for all times the pre-requisites to the full establishment of a New Testament Church.

After declaring the death, burial and resurrection of Jesus Christ, the Son of God, conviction settled upon the crowd. They were pricked, thoroughly stabbed [117] in their heart and cried out: "Men and brethren, what shall we do?" [118]

Peter's reply is clear and plain. "Repent, and be baptized every one of you in the name of Jesus Christ for the remission of sins, and ye shall receive the gift of the Holy Ghost." [119]

---

[117] Thompson's Chain Reference Bible, Acts 2:37, p.126, with **The Amplified New Testament**, Zondervan Pub., House. Grand Rapids, Michigan, 1958.

[118] Thompson's Chain Reference Bible, Acts 2:37, p.126

[119] Thompson's Chain Reference Bible, Acts 2:38, p.126

The response was immediate. About 3000 souls received the Word of the Gospel, repented, believed and were baptized. Thus the Lord added to His Church.

The two outstanding things to note here in this vital Sermon, at the founding of the Church, are these:

1. The call to repentance, then Baptism by immersion; and

2. Baptism in the Name of Jesus Christ.

There is absolutely no mention or quotation of the Command of Jesus as recorded in Matthew's Gospel as to "baptize in the Name of the Father, and of the Son, and of the Holy Ghost." He tells that God hath made this same JESUS both LORD and CHRIST, or, the LORD — JESUS — CHRIST, and calls on them to repent and be baptized in that Name. [120]

We would ask why Peter does this? It is the most important Sermon, the inaugural Sermon, for the New Testament Church. Had Peter but quoted Matthew Chapter 28 and verse 19, it would have settled forever the area of controversy which has arisen over the words of a Formula to be used in Baptism.

B. IN SAMARIA

The next instance in which Water Baptism is recorded is that which took place under the ministry of Philip in the city of Samaria. This account is given to us in Acts Chapter 8.

The Church at Jerusalem came under a time of persecution which caused the disciples to be scattered everywhere, scattering the Seed of the Word of the Gospel. Philip, one of the original seven, went down to Samaria and preached Christ unto them. [121] Signs and wonders followed the preaching according to the Lord's promise in the Gospel of Mark. [122]

The Scripture tells us: "When they believed Philip preaching the things concerning the Kingdom of God and the Name of Jesus Christ,

---

[120] *Ibid,* Acts 2:36,38, p.126
[121] *Ibid,* Acts 6:5; 21:8, p.130,150
[122] *Ibid,* Mark 16:15-18, p.58

they were baptized, both men and women." [123]

Here we see the pre-requisites of faith followed by Water Baptism. Further, the Scripture adds that they were "baptized in the Name of the Lord Jesus." [124]

Again it is to be noticed that there is no mention or quotation of the Command of Jesus as in the 'Great Commission'. The 'Trinitarian Formula' for Baptism is not referred to. They were baptized in the Name of the Lord Jesus.

The main points to be seen are as in the previous account of Baptism.

1. Water Baptism followed faith, and was by immersion; and

2. Water Baptism was administered in the Name of the Lord Jesus.

C. IN GAZA DESERT

Philip's ministry extended beyond Samaria. In Acts Chapter 8 and verse 26 through 40, the details of Philip's personal evangelism are given.

The Angel of the Lord directed Philip to leave Samaria and go toward the desert of Gaza. As he travelled, there was a man from Ethiopia, a man of great authority under Candace Queen of the Ethiopians, returning in his chariot from Jerusalem to his own country. Having been to Jerusalem, he was returning home hungry of heart for the God of Israel. The Spirit told Philip to join himself to the chariot. The Ethiopian, as was the custom, was reading the Scriptures out aloud, reading the great Messianic Chapter of the Prophet Isaiah, Chapter 53. Philip asked him did he understand what he was reading. He gave Philip a negative answer, inviting Philip to join him up in the chariot.

As they journeyed on, Philip "preached unto him Jesus." [125] This "preaching of Jesus" must have included the whole Gospel, for, as they came to certain water, the Eunuch asked Philip if there was

---

[123] Thompson's Chain Reference Bible, Acts 8:12, p.133

[124] *Ibid,* Acts 8:12, p.133

[125] Thompson's Chain Reference Bible, Acts 8:35, p.133

anything that hindered him being baptized? Upon the Eunuch's confession of faith in Jesus Christ as the Son of God, both he and Philip went down into the water and he was baptized.

Once again there is no mention of the Formula as given in the 'Great Commission'. Baptism is administered here:

1. By immersion in water; and

2. Upon confession of faith in Jesus Christ as the Son of God.

D. IN DAMASCUS

In Acts Chapter 9 we have the account of Saul's conversion on the road to Damascus. In due time he would be known as the Apostle Paul.

The Lord arrested Saul in the midst of his mad persecutions against the believers. As he is enroute to Damascus with letters of authority from the High Priest to bind many that were of 'The Way', both men and women; a supernatural light shone from heaven. This light was the very outshining of the glorified Son of God, Jesus Christ. As Saul fell to the earth he heard the voice of the Lord calling to him? "Saul, Saul, why persecutest thou Me?" Saul recognized that this was a Divine visitation, that the Lord was appearing to him. As God appeared to Moses in the burning bush and called to him, so the Lord was appearing here and calling to Saul. "Who art Thou, LORD?" Saul replied. [126]

Undoubtedly Saul thought he was speaking to the God of the Old Testament, that is, the LORD God.

No wonder he began to tremble with astonishment when the voice said: "I am JESUS whom thou persecutest: it is hard for thee to kick against the pricks." [127]

At this moment Saul was converted, born from above, for he called Jesus 'LORD', and "no man can say that JESUS is THE LORD but by the Holy Spirit." [128]

---

[126] *Ibid,* Acts 9:5, p.134
[127] *Ibid,* Acts 9:5, p.134
[128] Thompson's Chain Reference Bible, I Corinthians 12:3, p.183

Blinded by the Shekinah Glory of the risen and exalted Lord Jesus, Saul is led by the hand into Damascus, there to await instructions and directions as to the will of the Lord for his life.

As he was fasting 3 days and 3 nights without food or water, he received a vision of a man, Ananias, coming in, laying his hands on him in order that he might receive his sight. The Lord always works by His Spirit at both ends, and thus we find that Ananias receives a corresponding vision.

Ananias comes in obedience to the vision, lays hands on Saul, and as he did so, scales fell from Saul's eyes and his sight was restored. He receives the Holy Spirit, and in the process Ananias calls on Saul to be baptized.

In the account of Saul's conversion in Acts Chapter 22, and verse 16, he recalls the words of Ananias: "And now, why tarriest thou? arise and be baptized, and wash away thy sins, calling on the Name of the Lord."

Thus again, the emphasis is placed upon obedience to the command of Water Baptism. Saul is baptized, as a believer, in the Name of the Lord Jesus Christ. Once more there is no allusion to or any quotation of the 'Trinitarian Formula', but simply to the fact of Baptism "calling on the Name of the Lord", that is, in the Name of the Lord Jesus Christ.

E. IN CAESAREA

The next account of Baptism is found in Acts Chapter 10. Here the Holy Spirit through Luke the beloved physician records that which took place under Peter's ministry to the Gentiles in the house of Cornelius. It was to Peter that the Lord Jesus committed "the keys of the Kingdom" when He foretold the building of His Church. [129]

It is Peter who is expressly and specifically chosen as the channel in the Book of Acts to use these "Keys of the Kingdom", to open the Door of Faith, first to the Jews (Acts 2), and then to the Gentiles (Acts 10-11). Once again the risen Head of the Church, working by His Spirit at both ends, brings both ends together in due time.

---

[129] *Ibid*, Matthew 16:16-18, p.20

As Cornelius, a Centurian of the Italian Band, is praying to God, an angel appears to him in a vision assuring him that his prayers have been heard. The Angel gives him exact instructions and details by which he is to send men to Joppa and bring the Apostle Peter to his house telling him that Peter would give them "words, whereby he and all his house would be saved." [130]

He obeys immediately. At the other end, in Joppa, the Lord is working through a vision given to Peter. In the vision Peter sees a sheet let down from heaven to earth with all sorts of unclean creatures on it. A voice commands him to rise, kill and eat. Peter, steeped in Hebrew food-laws, refuses to do so. He does not as yet perceive the mind of the Spirit. This vision is repeated three times, for, "in the mouth of two or three witnesses shall every word be established." [131]

As Peter meditates on the vision, "The Spirit said unto him, Behold three men seek thee, arise therefore and get thee down, and go with them, doubting nothing, for I have sent them." [132]

Peter accompanies the men, with six of his own Jewish brethren, to the house of Cornelius. The Lord has to deal with his nationalistic sectarian attitude as he stands before the Gentiles. Hence, as Peter preached the Word of the Gospel, the Holy Spirit fell on all who heard the Word, and the evidence was seen and heard, as at Pentecost on the Jews, in that the Gentiles began to speak with other tongues. [133]

The Scripture account records: "Then answered Peter, Can any man forbid water that these should not be baptized, which have received the Holy Spirit as well as we? And he **commanded** them to be baptized in the Name of the Lord." [134]

Peter had to admit that as the Lord Jesus had baptized the Gentiles in the Spirit, then he could not refuse to baptize them in water, for one was the completeness of the other.

However, this was the exception, not the rule, in the Acts. God did

---

[130] Thompson's Chain Reference Bible, Acts 11:14, p.137
[131] *Ibid*, II Corinthians 13:1, p.197
[132] *Ibid*, Acts 10:19,20, p.136
[133] *Ibid*, Acts 10:46, p.137
[134] Thompson's Chain Reference Bible, Acts 10:48, p.137

this in order to deal with the nationalistic, sectarian attitude and spirit of the early believers and bring the Gentiles into the One Church, the Body of Christ.[135]

In summary, the same two facts are seen here as in each of the previous accounts.

1. Baptism for the Gentiles, as seen for the Jews, was by immersion in water, and

2. Water Baptism was commanded in the Name of the Lord. It was not 'an optional'. Let it be noted again that there is no reference here to the Trinitarian Formula.

F. IN PHILIPPI

Acts Chapter 16 furnishes us with the next account of Water Baptism.

Paul and Silas came from Troas into Philippi, a city of Macedonia, after a vision from the Lord. In the course of ministry there, a damsel with a spirit of divination (python) was delivered in the Name of Jesus Christ. The business men who used the damsel were aroused, causing an uproar in the city, the end result being that Paul and Silas were cast into prison. However, "all things work together for good", according to Romans Chapter 8 and verse 28. At the midnight hour, they prayed and sang praise to God. God sent an earthquake to the prison; the foundations were shaken, and all the prisoners bands were loosed, and all the doors were opened. The penalty of death was upon any Prison-keeper who lost his prisoners.

The keeper of the prison was about to kill himself thinking that all the prisoners had escaped. Paul and Silas assured him that they were all there. The jailor, under conviction, cried out: "Sirs, what must I do to be saved? And they said, Believe on the LORD JESUS CHRIST and thou shalt be saved, and thy house." [136]

What was the result? The jailor and all his house believed and were baptized straightway.[137]

---

135 *Ibid*, I Corinthians 12:13, p.183
136 Thompson's Chain Reference Bible, Acts 16:30,31, p.144
137 *Ibid*, Acts 16:32-34, p.144

No reference is to be found to any Formula of Matthew's Gospel. They believed on the Lord Jesus Christ and were baptized in water, believing in God.

So far, in Acts, Peter the Apostle, Philip the Evangelist, Ananias the disciple, and now the Apostle Paul, have not referred to or quoted the Command of Jesus recorded in the 'Great Commission'. They simply baptized repentant, believing persons in water by immersion, in the Name of the Lord Jesus, or Jesus Christ, or the Lord.

G. IN CORINTH

The seventh particular reference to Water Baptism is found in Acts Chapter 18, under Paul's ministry at Corinth.

After Paul left Athens, he came to Corinth. He reasoned in the Synagogues with the Jews and Greeks out of the Scriptures, persuading them that Jesus of Nazareth was indeed the Christ of God, the Saviour of the world.

After being opposed by the blasphemy of the Jews, he shook his raiment, declaring to the unbelieving Jews that their blood would be upon their own heads, and from now he would go to the Gentiles. Paul then entered into the house of Justus, whose house joined hard to the Synagogue. Crispus, the Chief Ruler of the Synagogue, believed on the Lord with all his house, and the Scriptures declare: "Many of the Corinthians hearing believed, and were baptized."[138]

Though no details beyond this are given in Acts, in the Epistle to the Corinthians, Paul reminds them of his coming to Corinth and the establishment of the Church there. He reminds them that they should not be divided over names and personalities, beseeching them by the Name of the LORD JESUS CHRIST to speak the same thing, and have one mind, and one judgment. Then he refers them to their Baptism by saying? "Is Christ divided? was Paul crucified for you? or were ye baptized in the name of Paul? I thank God that I baptized none of you, but Crispus and Gaius; lest any should say that I had baptized in mine own name."[139]

---

[138] *Ibid,* Acts 18:8, p.146
[139] Thompson's Chain Reference, I Corinthians 1:13-15, p.174,175

The implications of this will be considered later on. It is sufficient for the present to see once more the main emphasis in each record of Baptism in Acts. That is:

1. Water Baptism was by immersion in water, after a person believed, and,

2. Water Baptism was administered in the Name of the Lord Jesus Christ. Once again there is total absence of any quotation of any Formula, or Matthew 28:19.

H. IN EPHESUS

The final record of Baptism in the Acts is that which took place in Ephesus, and again, this is under the ministry of the Apostle Paul. The details are supplied for us in Acts Chapter 19, and verses 1 through 7.

Paul found certain disciples at Ephesus. As he began to minister to them, in the spirit he sensed that something — Someone — was absent. He immediately questioned them as to the matter of their Baptism. He asked them had they received the Holy Spirit? They replied that they did not even know that the Holy Spirit had been given. Now if these disciples had been baptized in "the Name of the Father, and of the Son, and of the Holy Ghost" they would at least have 'heard' of the Holy Ghost. However, this was not so. Paul continues: "Unto what (or who) were ye baptized? And they said, Unto John's Baptism." Then Paul declares to them the difference between John's Baptism and Christian Baptism. This difference will be explained in the proper section. When the Ephesians heard this "they were baptized in the Name of the Lord Jesus."[140]

The Holy Spirit sealed this act of Paul and Baptism in the Name of the Lord Jesus, by coming upon these Ephesians in the laying on of hands, for they spake with tongues and prophesied.

In summary of this section presently under consideration, it is to be seen that there was something inadequate, something lacking in John's Baptism, even though it was by immersion. Under Paul the Apostle, these Ephesian believers were re-immersed to complete that which was insufficient in the Baptism of John.

---

[140] Thompson's Chain Reference, Acts 19:4,5, p.147

Once again we conclude:

1. Water Baptism is by immersion, and for the believing, and
2. Water Baptism is administered in the Name of the Lord.

In concluding our findings on Water Baptism as in the Book of Acts let us bring into focus that which each records reveals.

1. **In Jerusalem,** Baptism was for the repentant, and by immersion in the Name of Jesus Christ.
2. **In Samaria,** Baptism was for the believing, by immersion, in the Name of the Lord Jesus.
3. **In Gaza Desert,** Baptism was for the believing, upon confession of faith in the Lord Jesus as the Son of God.
4. **In Damascus,** Baptism was by immersion for the believing Saul, calling on the Name of the Lord.
5. **In Caesarea,** Water Baptism was by immersion, and commanded to be administered in the Name of the Lord.
6. **In Philippi,** Baptism was by immersion, as the jailor and his house believed in the Lord Jesus Christ, believing in God.
7. **In Corinth,** Baptism was by immersion, not in the Name of Paul, but in the Name of the Lord Jesus Christ.
8. **In Ephesus,** the Baptism of John was redundant, lacking that which was vital to the New Testament Church, and so the Ephesians were re-immersed under Paul and in the Name of the Lord Jesus.

Therefore, not one of the eight records of Baptism in Acts show Baptism to be by sprinkling, nor is there any quotation of the Formula of Matthew 28:19, but each account shows Baptism by immersion, and always in the Name of the Lord, the Lord Jesus, or Jesus Christ. This was only for those who had experienced the necessary pre-requisites of repentance from dead works and faith towards God through Christ.

(Note:— Various translations as the Revised Version, the King James, Lamsa Translation, The Douay Version, and others, show Baptism to be in the Name of the "Lord Jesus", "Jesus Christ", "Lord", and various have the full Triune Name "The Lord Jesus Christ". Early MSS show that the proper use was the Triune Name and not just a part or parts of the Name.[141]

---

[141] Hall, William Phillips, **A Remarkable Biblical Discovery,** or, '**The Name' of God according to the Scriptures.** American Tract Society, 7 West 45th Street, New York, U.S.A. 1931. p.69-76

CHAPTER 7:

WATER BAPTISM IN THE EPISTLES

APOSTOLIC INTERPRETATION OF BAPTISM

It is evident from the commands concerning Baptism as given in the Gospels, and the accounts of the fulfilment of those commands as in the Book of Acts, that there seems to be a great discrepancy. The discrepancy is particularly centered around 'the Formula' to be administered in Baptism.

Why did the Lord Jesus command the disciples to "Baptize in the Name of the Father, and of the Son, and of the Holy Ghost", yet nearly every record or reference to Baptism, both in the Acts and in the Epistles, is spoken of as Baptism "in or into the Name of the Lord, the Lord Jesus, or Jesus Christ, or the Lord — Jesus — Christ", depending on various translations.

We are forced to ask some pertinent questions in order to find some reconcilable answer. Did the disciples disobey the command of Jesus? Did they misunderstand His command? Why did they never quote the Command of Matthew 28:19 in administering Baptism? Why did they always baptize in the Name of the Lord Jesus Christ? Why is there no exact 'Formula' used in the New Testament? Is there some mistake? Is there some contradiction between the Gospels and the Acts? Or, does it really matter what the disciples did in Acts, or should we really just quote the Command of Jesus from the Gospel of Matthew? Do words really matter at all, if the person who is being baptized has a heart that is right before God and is in obedience to the Word? Is the **act of obedience** in Baptism by immersion more important than any **words of a Formula**?

These and other related questions naturally arise as one studies the Doctrine of Baptisms both in the Gospels and Acts. Can these things be reconciled? Endless strife and division has resulted out of an endeavor to reconcile the Gospels with the Acts.

The Gospels have been pitted against the Acts and the Acts

against the Gospels. Jesus has been made to contradict Peter, and Peter to contradict Jesus. The Apostles have been made to contradict each other. All of this need not be so. The writer of this thesis believes that there is no contradiction between the Command of Jesus and the obedience of the Apostles. Both the Gospels and the Acts belong to each other.

The premise of the following comments is that "**the Book of Acts is the Apostolic interpretation, by the Spirit, of the Great Commission and the Commands of Jesus in the Gospels.**" This is to say, the Great Commission of the Gospels must be interpreted in the light of the Book of Acts.

Let us see the validity of these statements.

The Great Commission or the Commission of Jesus to the Early Church is to be found in the following table of Scriptures.

1. Matthew Chapter 28:18-20;

2. Mark Chapter 16:15-18;

3. Luke Chapter 24:47-49

4. John Chapter 20:21-23,30,31;

5. Acts Chapter 1:2,8.

All of these Scriptures together constitute "The Commission" of Jesus, for some things are mentioned in one Gospel that are not mentioned in another, and so all these Scriptures together must be considered as involving "The Whole Commission" of Jesus to the disciples.

The Commission as given in these Scriptures, was given **after** the DEATH, BURIAL AND RESURRECTION of the Lord Jesus and just **before** His ASCENSION, EXALTATION to the Father's Right Hand, and **prior** to the Day of Pentecost, when the Holy Spirit was poured out on the waiting disciples, waiting to fulfil the Commission.

As we study the Book of Acts we discover exactly **how** the disciples interpreted the Commission and the Commandments therein. Taking the Commission as in Mark's Gospel, we find the emphasis therein upon preaching the Gospel to every creature, people believing and being baptized, and signs following the believers.

These signs included speaking with new tongues, laying hands on the sick for their recovery, taking up deadly serpents and not being harmed by them, and drinking deadly poison and being preserved through it all. Jesus said all of this would be done in HIS NAME.

Now if we desire to know what Jesus meant by "speaking with new tongues" in Mark's Gospel (even though some count these verses spurious), then where do we go? The answer: To the Book of Acts. There in Acts we read the story of the believers who spoke with new or other tongues as the Spirit gave them utterance.[142]

Acts is the interpretation of this part of Mark's Gospel. Again, if we desire to understand what Jesus meant in Mark when He spoke of "laying hands on the sick, and taking up deadly serpents", once more we turn to the Book of Acts, and there we see the interpretation of what Jesus meant. Acts gives an illustration of Paul laying hands on the sick, and taking up a deadly serpent, yet he is unharmed.[143] Thus Mark's Gospel is interpreted for us in the Acts.

Let us take up Luke's Gospel and the area of the Commission as given there. The emphasis in the Commission as in Luke is upon "repentance and remissions of sins being preached in HIS NAME." There is no specific reference to 'repentance and remission of sins' in Matthew's Gospel or Mark's Gospel in the Commission. This is the emphasis in Luke.

Hence, if we want to know how the disciples interpreted the Commission as in Luke, we turn to the Book of Acts. There we see how the Apostles preached repentance and remission of sins in and through the Name of the Lord Jesus Christ.[144]

The same consistency of interpretation is found in Acts regarding "believing in HIS NAME" as in John's Gospel.[145]

We now consider and apply the same principle as above to the

---

[142] Thompson's Chain Reference Bible, Acts 2:4; 10:46,47; 19:4-6
[143] *Ibid*, Acts 28:1-6, 7-9, p.159
[144] *Ibid*, Luke 24:47-49; Acts 2:38, p.96,126
[145] *Ibid*, John 20:30,31; Acts 3:16, p.122,127

Great Commission as recorded in Matthew's Gospel and as in interpreted in the light of the Book of Acts.

The Book of Acts is the only infallible account that we have of how the Apostles interpreted the Commission of Jesus in the Gospels. Hence we need not depend primarily on the History Books or the Traditions of men, or Church History. The Acts of the Apostles stands in its own Divine light as the interpretation of the Great Commission.

Consistency of interpretation therefore demands that, if we want to know what Jesus meant when He said in Matthew 28, verse 19, to "Baptize in the Name of the Father, of the Son, of the Holy Ghost", then we must turn to the Book of Acts. Both Gospels and Acts go together. The Gospels cannot be used at the expense of the Acts, nor the Acts at the expense of the Gospels. The words of the Lord Jesus cannot be used against the words of the Apostles.

Therefore, we have seen that the Gospels command that Baptism be in the Name of the Father, Son and Holy Ghost, and the Acts show Baptism in the Name of the Lord — Jesus — Christ.

There is but one conclusion to come to and that is this. The Apostolic interpretation of "The Name of the Father, Son and Holy Ghost" is found in "The Name of the Lord Jesus Christ."

There is nothing wrong with Matthew Chapter 28:19. This Command was given by the Holy Spirit through Jesus, according to Acts Chapter 1 and verse 2.

There is nothing wrong with Acts Chapter 2 and verse 36 through 38. Peter gave this command when he was filled with the Spirit.

BOTH Scriptures can be rightly used, for both were inspired by the same Holy Spirit.

It is worthy to remember that the Baptismal Command demands the use of a TRIUNE NAME, and that is, "THE NAME" (not Names!) of the Father, and of the Son, and of the Holy Spirit.

The only TRIUNE NAME in the whole revelation of God is that in the New Testament, in THE NAME of the LORD JESUS CHRIST.

It is unthinkable that the Apostles disobeyed the Command of the Lord Jesus. If this is questioned, then may every other foundational truth be questioned, for these are declared by the same Apostles.

No Doctrine of Scripture can be established on one verse only, but in the mouth of two or three witnessing Scriptures. Scripture must interpret Scripture.

We have before us the **one** Scripture Command of Jesus to Baptize in the Name of the Father, Son, and Holy Spirit, and then we have about **twelve** (or fourteen) on Baptism in the Name of the Lord Jesus Christ. Therefore the twelve or fourteen Scriptures must be taken as the interpretation of the one Scripture, and this is exactly the case.

The Command of Peter in Acts for Baptism in the Name of the Lord Jesus Christ is the interpretation of the Command of Jesus for Baptism in the Name of the Father, Son and Holy Spirit, as in Matthew, and it is to be understood this way when invoked in Water Baptism.

The reason that Matthew 28:19 is not specifically used or even quoted in the Acts is this. **One does not fulfil a Command by merely quoting it!** The Apostles did not **quote** the Command; they **obeyed** it!

There is no reconciliation between the Gospels and the Acts if this is not so. If the record of Acts be mistaken here, and does not mean this, then what do words mean?

It is sometimes contended that "In the Name of . . ." simply means, "On the authority of . . ." The answer to this is seen in the use of the Greek prepositions.

There is the Greek preposition $\epsilon\pi\iota$, meaning "upon, over", and $\epsilon\nu$, meaning "in", or "by", and there is $\epsilon\iota\varsigma$ meaning "into, unto", and the Greek translations use either of these words when speaking of Baptism 'in' or 'into' or 'upon' the Name of the Lord Jesus Christ.[146]

J. F. & Brown Commentary, on Matthew 28:19 remarks:

"Go ye therefore and teach all nations . . . rather, 'make disciples of all nations,' for, 'teaching' in the more usual sense of that word, comes in afterward, and is expressed by a different term . . . Baptizing them **in** the Name . . . it should be '**into** the Name' as in I Corinthians 10:2, 'And they

---

[146] Berry, George Ricker, **The Interlinear Greek-English New Testament**, K.J.V. Zondervan Publishing House, Grand Rapids, Michigan, U.S.A. 1972. Matthew 28:19; Acts 2:38; p.87,316

were baptized **unto** (rather "**into**") Moses, and Galatians 3:27,' 'For as many of you as have been baptized **into** Christ' . . ."[147]

(emphasis mine).

This Section concludes with our premise. The Book of Acts is the Apostolic interpretation, by the Spirit, and the fulfilment of the Commission of Jesus as given in the Gospels, and this is so with regard to every fundamental truth of the Gospel; that is, repentance, faith, Water Baptism in the Name of the Eternal Godhead, as well as Baptism in the Holy Spirit.

Water Baptism is 'upon the authority of' and 'into the Name of' the Lord Jesus Christ.

THE SPIRITUAL SIGNIFICANCE OF BAPTISM

Having considered Water Baptism in the Gospels, and in the Acts, we proceed to understand the revelation of Baptism as in the Church Epistles.

It is appropriate at the beginning of this Section to recognize the difference in the significance of Baptism as laid out in the Gospels, the Acts and the Epistles. As in other fundamental Doctrines of the Faith "once delivered to the saints"[148] so it is in regard to the Doctrine of Baptisms. There is a progressive revelation and unfolding of the truth in the Gospels, the Acts and the Epistles; and in order to receive the complete view and perceive the fulness of truth all these groupings are necessary to each other.

We cannot understand the full significance or truth of Baptism only by that which is supplied in the Gospels.

Nor can we get the full orb of truth of Baptism only by that set forth in the Acts of the Apostles. The same holds true as to the Epistles. The Gospels, the Acts and the Epistles are all needed to give to us a full and balanced truth as relates to this subject. The difference is seen in the following brief remarks.

---

[147] Jamieson, Robert Rev. D. D., Faussett, A. R. AM., Brown, David, Rev, D.D., **Commentary Critical & Explanatory on the Whole Bible,** Zondervan Publishing House, Grand Rapids, Michigan, U.S.A. p.63

[148] Thompson's Chain Reference Bible, Jude 3, p.253

1. The Gospels especially record the **Commands** of Jesus.

2. The Acts particularly give the **fulfilment** of these Commands by the Baptism of the repentant and believing.

3. The Epistles especially bring out the very essence and the **inner spiritual truth** of Baptism. This is not to be found expressly in the Gospels or the Acts as clearly as it is set forth in the Epistles. This same principle holds true as pertaining to the Lord's Table. In the Gospels we see the Lord instituting the Table by His own Body and Blood of the New Covenant. In the Acts we see the Early Church meeting together, and "breaking bread" the first day of the week. In the Epistles is given the true essence of Communion, the inner and spiritual truth of the Table, which is not found in the Gospels and to Acts.[149]

All of this is given to the Church by the Apostle Paul, and without it, there would be lacking much truth concerning the Table, as well as Baptism.

The same is true concerning the death, burial and resurrection of the Lord. These things are recorded for us **factually** in the Gospels. These things are **preached** in the Book of Acts. However, it is in the Epistles that these things are **interpreted** for us, as to the very heart, the very essence, the inner and spiritual significance of that which took place at Calvary. This is true of many other things. The same is true of Water Baptism.

Without the Epistles, we would not have the inner and spiritual reality of Baptism as commanded by Christ in the Gospels and obeyed in Acts. The Epistles (the spirit) interpret the Acts (the soul), as the Acts interpret the Gospels (the flesh-body).

A. INVOCATION OF THE NAME OF THE GODHEAD

Water Baptism in its inner spiritual meaning is, first of all, Baptism into the Name of the Father, of the Son, of the Holy Spirit. In other words, it is Baptism into the Name of the Eternal Godhead. It is also

---

[149] Thompson's Chain Reference Bible, Matthew 26:26-28; Acts 20:7; Acts 2:42-47; I Corinthians 11:23-34, p.32,149,126,182,183

Baptism in the Name of the Lord Jesus Christ. This is seen by combining the Command of Jesus in Matthew with the obedience of the Apostles in Acts.

1. What does it mean to be baptized into the Name of the Father, and of the Son, and of the Holy Ghost? That is, into the Name of the Eternal Godhead.

   Kenyon says:

   > "When we are baptized into the Name of the Father, it gives us the place of a child and all the privileges of a child, all the inheritance and wealth of the child.
   >
   > We are baptized into the protection and care and fellowship of the God of the universe as our Father — We take on all that union means.
   >
   > We have the standing of a Son, the privilege of a Son, the responsibilities of a Son. We have become by that baptism a joint heir with Jesus, and an heir of God . . .
   >
   > When we are baptized into the Name of the Holy Spirit, we are baptized into the Name, wealth, power, wisdom, and glory of God's representative on the earth — all the Spirit has we are baptized into."[150]

2. What does it mean to be baptized into the Name of the Lord Jesus Christ? It has been seen already how the Apostolic interpretation of the Name of the Father, Son, and Holy Ghost is fulfilled in the Name of the Lord Jesus Christ. The Name of the Lord Jesus Christ is the Name of the Godhead BODILY.

   As it has pleased the Father that in the Son all fulness should dwell, so the Fulness of the GODHEAD NAME is in the Son. It is not that the Son is the Father, nor the Holy Spirit, for, the Father is eternally the Father, the Son is eternally the Son, and the Holy Spirit is the Holy Spirit eternally. But in the redemptive plan it has pleased God that in the Son all the Fulness dwell. The Son is the FULNESS of the GODHEAD — BODILY![151]

---

[150] Kenyon, E. W., **The Wonderful Name of Jesus,** Kenyon's Gospel Publishing House, 528 Weste Amerige, Fullerton, California, U.S.A. 1927. p.57

[151] Thompson's Chain Reference Bible, Colossians 1:19; 2:9, p.211

Because this is so, the Fulness of the Godhead Name dwells in Him; that is, "The NAME of the FATHER, and of the SON, and of the HOLY SPIRIT" is completely expressed in Him. This is seen in the Name of the Lord Jesus Christ. It is "The Family Name", of which Pauls writes: "For this cause I bow my knees unto the Father of our LORD JESUS CHRIST of whom **the whole family** in heaven and earth is Named."[152]

What then is it to be baptized into the Name of the Lord Jesus Christ?

Once more we quote from E. W. Kenyon. He writes:

"When a believer is baptized into the Name of the Lord Jesus he puts on the Lord Jesus . . . Baptizing into the Name of the Lord Jesus Christ is even richer and fuller than either of these — it comprehends all that is in them with additions. When I am baptized into Christ, I put on Christ . . . Baptism in this sense is equivalent to marriage. When the wife puts on marriage she take her husband's name and enters into her husband's possessions and has legal right to her husband's home. When the believer is baptized into the Name of Christ, he puts on all that is in Christ. He not only puts on the Name but takes his legal rights and his privileges in Christ."[153]

Paul says to the Colossians, "we are buried with Him by baptism", (Colossians 2:12), and to the Galatians (Galatians 3:27), "As many as have been baptized into Christ have put on Christ", and yet again to the Romans (Romans 6:3-4), "As many of us as were baptized into Jesus Christ have been baptized into His death . . ."

To the Corinthians (I Corinthians 1:10-17) Paul writes beseeching them "by the Name of the Lord Jesus Christ" that they all speak the same thing, be joined togehter in the same mind and the same judgment. He reminds them that they were not baptized into "the name of Paul" but into the Name of the One who was crucified for them, that is, the Lord Jesus Christ.

James, writing to the Strangers scattered abroad says: "Do not they blaspheme that worthy Name by the which ye are called?"[154] The

---

[152] *Ibid,* Ephesians 3:14,15, p.204
[153] Kenyon, E. W., **The Wonderful Name of Jesus,** p.59
[154] Thompson's Chain Reference Bible, James 2:7, p.239

Amplified translates this by: "That precious Name by which you are distinguished and called (**The Name of Christ invoked in Baptism**)."[155] (emphasis mine)

The Apostle Peter, writing also the Strangers scattered abroad refers to baptism, "The like figure whereunto even baptism doth also now save us (not the putting away of the filth of the flesh, but the answer of a good conscience toward God,) by the resurrection of Jesus Christ: . . ."[156]

The Name is always significant of the Nature in Bible days. To be baptized into the Name of the Father, Son, and Holy Spirit is to be baptized into the Name of the Eternal Godhead and all that belongs in the redemptive plan. To be baptized into the Name of the Lord Jesus Christ is to be baptized into the Family Name, and into the Name of the Fulness of the Godhead Bodily. It is be baptized into the New Nature which belongs by right of New Birth to the New Creature.

Lucy P. Knott states this truth beautifully in her Booklet, "The Triune Name."

"Only the Triune God could conceive such a Name; presenting the Persons of the Trinity in three names — Father, Son and Holy Ghost; and then in the New Testament showing forth the Trinity in one Name — the Lord Jesus Christ.

Let us give a brief resume of the introduction of the previous chapters.

(1) The Name "Lord" shows forth the wisdom, foreknowledge and love of the Father. This wisdom, foreknowledge and love, he hides in the Son for the execution of all His plans and purposes. The Name "Lord" also identifies the Son as the Jehovah of the Old Testament.

(2) The Name "Jesus" shows forth the humility, humanity, sufferings and example of the Son, who is made the visible active agent of the Godhead.

(3) The Name "Christ" shows forth the power of the Holy Ghost. This power was poured out upon the Son "without measure" for the execution of the Father's eternal plans and purposes."[157]

---

[155] Amplified New Testament, James 2:7

[156] Thompson's Chain Reference Bible, 1 Peter 3:21, p.244

[157] Knott, Lucy P., **The Triune Name,** Nazarene Publishing House, 2923 Troost Ave., Kansas City, Missouri, U.S.A. 1937. p.30,31

Thus Baptism in the Name of the Eternal Godhead in the Name of the Lord Jesus Christ brings to us the Fulness of the Godhead and all that was wrought for us by the Father, the Son and the Holy Spirit.

B. IDENTIFICATION WITH CHRIST

Not only is the repentant and believing baptized in water, having the Name of the Godhead Bodily invoked upon him, there is further truth shown in the Epistles relative to this Ordinance.

This is seen in the Scriptures under consideration here, all of which show that the believer is **identified** with the Lord Jesus Christ in His death, burial and resurrection.

1. The believer is identified with His **Death**:

   "Know ye not that so many of us as were baptized into Jesus Christ have been baptized into His DEATH?"

2. The believer is identified with His **Burial**:

   "Therefore we are BURIED with Him by baptism into death . . ."

3. The believer is identified with His **Resurrection**:

   "That like as Christ was RAISED UP from the dead by the glory of the Father, even so we also should walk in newness of life."[158]

As the Lord Jesus Christ became identified with us in His death, burial and resurrection, so the believer becomes identified with Him in Water Baptism in this same death, burial and resurrection. In fact, Christ refers to His own death as "a Baptism", as seen in the use of the Greek word $\beta\alpha\pi\tau\iota\sigma\theta\eta\nu\alpha\iota$, thus Baptism is linked with His death, burial and resurrection.[159]

The 'going down' of the Candidate into the water is the symbol of the 'going down into death'; identification with Christ's death. The immersion, submersion of the Candidate 'beneath the water' is identification with His burial. This is why sprinkling cannot fulfil the significance of Baptism. Only Baptism by immersion, or submersion

---

[158] Thompson's Chain Reference Bible, Romans 6:3,4, p.164
[159] Kittel, Gerhard, **Theological Dictionary of the N.T.** Vol. 1., Wm. B. Eerdmans Publishing Co., Grand Rapids, Michigan, U.S.A. p.537, with Mark 10:38; Luke 12:50

demonstrates or illustrates this truth. The 'rising up' out of the water signifies the believer's resurrection, rising up to walk in newness of life in Christ. It is identification with the resurrection of Christ.

The Article of Faith by the Baptists puts it this way: XXXIX,

"Baptism is an Ordinance of the New Testament, given by Christ, to be dispensed upon persons professing faith, or that are made disciples; who, upon profession of faith, ought to be baptized and after to partake of the Lord's Supper ... XL The way and manner of dispensing this Ordinance is dipping or plunging the body under water. It, being a sign, must answer the things signified; which is, that interest the saints have in the death, burial and resurrection of Christ; and that as certainly as the body is buried under water, and risen again, so certainly shall the bodies of the saints be raised by the power of Christ, in the day of the resurrection, to reign with Christ."[160]

C. INCORPORATION OF NEW COVENANT CIRCUMCISION

The final facet of truth which is given in the Epistles is that which concerns the believer being incorporated into the New Covenant. Water Baptism is the New Testament antitypical fulfilment of the Old Testament Rite of Circumcision. Abraham was given "The Covenant of Circumcision."[161]

There were three particular things involved in the Rite, each of which pointed, first to the work of the Cross, and then on through the Cross to the believer's experience in Water Baptism, which is New Covenant Circumcision. These things were:

1. The cutting away of the **flesh**, which also involved the shedding of **blood**. It pointed to the DEATH of the Lord Jesus Christ, for, when His Flesh and Blood were offered in sacrifice for us to God, He was indeed 'cut off' out of the land of the living for our sins and transgressions.[162]

---

[160] Bettenson, Henry, **Documents of the Christian Church,** Oxford University Press, New York, U.S.A. p.354

[161] Thompson's Chain Reference Bible, Acts 7:8, p.131

[162] Thompson's Chain Reference Bible, Isaiah 53:8, p.686

2. The second thing was that this Rite took place on the **eighth** day. Eight is significant of the number of resurrection. It pointed to the RESURRECTION of the Son of God on the eighth day, or, the first day of a new week.[163]

3. The third thing involved was the **invocation of the Name** of the child. This took place at the circumcision of the child. Though the Name was given at birth, it was not invoked until the day of his circumcision.[164]

   This pointed to THE NAME of the Godhead Bodily, the Fulness of the Divine Name as given to Jesus when He was made both Lord and Christ, or, The LORD JESUS CHRIST.[165]

All of these things are found in Genesis Chapter 17. Only when a Hebrew child had especially experienced these things involved in the Rite were they counted in Covenant relationship with God, and thus entitled to the blessings, the promises, the privileges and responsibilities of the Abrahamic Covenant.

The New Testament antitypical fulfilment of this is in New Testament or New Covenant Circumcision, Water Baptism. Paul in writing to the Colossians tells them: "In whom also ye are circumcised with the circumcision made without hands, in putting off the body of the sins of the flesh, by the circumcision of Christ: Buried with him in baptism, wherein also ye are risen with him **through the faith of the operation of God,** who raised him from the dead."[166]

In Water Baptism, the believer is identified with Christ's death. he is 'cut off' from the old life of sin, and this old life is buried with Christ. Water Baptism speaks of a circumcision of the heart, of the spirit, and not of the flesh.[167]

In Water Baptism, the believer has A NEW NAME invoked upon him, the Name of the Father, Son and Holy Spirit, which is interpreted in the Name of the Lord, in the Lord Jesus Christ, the Name of the

---

[163] *Ibid*, Matthew 28:1, p.36 N.T.

[164] *Ibid*, Genesis 17:12; 21:3,4, p.14,18. O.T.

[165] *Ibid*, Acts 2:36, p.126 N.T.

[166] Thompson's Chain Reference Bible, Colossians 2:12,13, p.211

[167] *Ibid*, Romans 2:28,29, p.162

Godhead Bodily.

In Water Baptism the Holy Spirit comes upon the Candidate so that he may rise to walk in newness of life. This is resurrection. The believer is now in New Covenant relationship with God through Christ, and is now entitled to all the blessings, promises, privileges and responsibilities of that Covenant.

All of this is inwrought by FAITH in the operation of God. The Holy Spirit working in us what was done for us at Calvary.

CHRISTIAN BAPTISM CONTRASTED WITH JOHN'S BAPTISM

In this Section we consider briefly the main points of contrast between John's Baptism and Christian Baptism. It is clear, as has already been mentioned, that John's Baptism was incomplete and inadequate for the New Testament Church. When Apollos came to Ephesus, Aquilla and Priscilla took him unto them and expounded the way of God more perfectly. The reason why this was so is found in the Scripture which says "they knew only the Baptism of John."[168] Apollos was humble enough to accept further teaching.

Later on Paul came to Ephesus and found about twelve disciples there, and as already seen in Acts Chapter 19 and verses 1 through 7, baptized them again, because they knew only John's Baptism.

What then are the basic differences between these Baptisms?

Let us see the similarities first, and then consider the differences.

John's Baptism involved repentance; so did Christian Baptism.

John's Baptism involved confession and remission of sins through faith in the coming Messiah. Christian Baptism involves confession and remission of sins through faith in Christ Jesus also.

John's Baptism was by immersion; so is Christian Baptism.

Thus in these main points, John's Baptism and Christian Baptism are similar.

Let us look at the differences.

John's Baptism was **before** the death, burial and resurrection of Christ.

---

[168] *Ibid*, Acts 18:25, p.147

Christian Baptism is **after** the death, burial and resurrection of Christ.

John's Baptism was **nameless.** Christian Baptism is into **the Name of the Eternal Godhead,** the Name of the Father, Son, and Holy Spirit, as interpreted in the Name of the Lord Jesus Christ.

Thus we see, that even though John's Baptism was blessed and ordained of God, it was inadequate for the New Testament Church. Christian Baptism fulfills that which was lacking in John's Baptism.

The very meaning of Christian Baptism is Baptism into the redemptive work of Christ; identification with Christ's death, burial and resurrection. This was not so in John's Baptism.

Then again, Christian Baptism involves the invocation of the Godhead Name; this was lacking in John's Baptism. It was not a matter of mere words of a powerless Formula to Paul. It was identification with Calvary and it was invocation of the Name of God. There is power in the proper use of 'The Name', whether for salvation, healing the sick, exorcism, prayer or Water Baptism. This is the difference between John's Baptism and Christian Baptism. Truly, as White says "recovery of the biblical doctrine of initiation would involve an altogether new emphasis upon the profound scriptural teaching about baptism into Christ, with the accompanying truth of the baptismal gift of the Spirit to every believer."[168/b]

[168/b] White, R. E. O., M.A., B.D., **The Biblical Doctrine of Initiation,** Wm. B. Eerdmans Publishing Co., Grand Rapids, Michigan, 1960, p.315

CHAPTER 8

SUMMARY AND CONCLUSION

The evidence before us brings us to our Summary and Conclusion.

Having considered the problem, tracing the history of Baptism, both in the Early Church and the Church Fathers, and having explored the various Tenets of Modern Theology as to Water Baptism, certain conclusions must be forthcoming.

In the light of the Doctrine of Baptism in the Gospels, the Acts and the Epistles, the questions with which we began our thesis find their answers, as to Form or Mode, as to Formula, and as to Apostolic interpretation of Baptism.

AS TO FORM OR MODE:

Water Baptism is by immersion, not sprinkling. Immersion, or submersion only sets forth properly the significance of Baptism as identification with Christ in His death, burial and resurrection.

AS TO FORMULA:

Or, as to words to be used in Baptism, the following would be a suitable one. To the Candidate, the one baptizing may say:
"Upon the confession of your faith, I baptize you into THE Name of the Father, and of the Son, and of the Holy Ghost; into THE Name of the Lord Jesus Christ; that like as Christ was raised from the dead by the glory of the Father, even so you also shall rise to walk in newness of life."

This Formula is simply grouping together three verses of Scripture, as set forth (1) In the Gospels, and (2) in the Acts, and (3) in the Epistles. This Formula **quotes** the Command of Jesus in Matthew Chapter 28:19. It **invokes** the Name of the Lord Jesus Christ as in the Book of Acts and it **declares** the spiritual significance of Baptism as in the Epistles.

"Whatsoever you do in **word or deed,** do all in the Name of the Lord Jesus."[169]

A Formula is not be looked upon as a group of 'magic words', or 'powerless meaningless words'. There is power and authority in that Name, whether used in the saving of souls, healing of the sick, casting out of devils, praying, or in the invocation of that Name as in Water Baptism. It is not merely quoting meaningless and powerless words of a Scripture Formula.

AS TO APOSTOLIC INTERPRETATION:

Water Baptism is clearly taught to be identification with the Son of God in His death, burial and resurrection; and, it is also New Covenant circumcision of the heart, an operation of God which takes place by faith in the Word and the Spirit of God.

Baptism involves the establishment of a Covenant of grace between God and the person baptized.[170] Though administered only once, Baptism is to be used by Christians throughout their whole life. Nowhere do the Apostles call on Christians to repeat their Baptism, however, they frequently recall to their minds Baptism once received.[171]

FINALLY, Water Baptism in all its related facets must be obeyed so that the believer will have "the answer of a good conscience towards God."[172] That is, not a conscience governed by itself, or the traditions of men, but a conscience which lines itself up by submission and obedience to the infallible Word and will of God.

AMEN AND AMEN

---

[169] Thompson's Chain Reference Bible, Colossians 3:17, p.212

[170] Pieper, Francis, **Christian Dogmatics,** Concordia Publishing House, Saint Louis, Missouri, U.S.A. 1953. p.275

[171] Ibid, p.276

[172] Thompson's Chain Reference Bible, 1 Peter 3:21, p.244

BIBLIOGRAPHY

1. Althanaus, Paul, **The Theology of Martin Luther**, Philadelphia, Fortress Press, 1966.

2. **Amplified New Testament**, Grand Rapids, Michigan, Zondervan Publishing House, 1958.

3. Bainton, Roland H., **Early Christianity**, Princeton, New Jersey, D. Van Nostrand Co. Inc., 1960.

4. Bettenson, Henry, **Documents of the Christian Church**, New York and London, Oxford University Press, 1954.

5. **Early Church Fathers**, The Library of Christian Classics, Vol. 1. Philadelphia, The Westminister Press.

6. Gregory, J. R., **The Theological Student**, 25-35 City Road, E. C. London, Charles H. Kelly, 1910.

7. Hall, William Phillips, **A Remarkable Biblical Discovery**, or, "The Name" of God according to the Scriptures, 45th Street, New York, American Tract Society, 1931.

8. Hammond, T. C., **In Understanding be Man**, Aylesbury, Bucks, Great Britain, Hazell Watson & Viney Ltd., 1971.

9. **Handbook of Doctrine**, International Headquarters, London, E. C. 4, The Salvation Army, 1940.

10. Jamieson, Faussett & Brown, **Commentary Critical & Explanatory on the Whole Bible**, Grand Rapids, Michigan, Zondervan Publishing House.

11. Kenyon, E. W., **The Wonderful Name of Jesus**, 528 Weste Amerige, Fullerton, California, Kenyon's Publishing Society, 1927.

12. Kittel, Gerhard, **Theological Dictionary of the New Testament**, Vol. 1, Grand Rapids, Michigan, Wm. B. Eerdmans Publishing Co., 1969.

13. Knott, Lucy P., **The Triune Name**, 2923 Troost Ave., Kansas City, Missouri, Nazarene Publishing House, 1937.

14. Oliver, Samuel, Rev., **Synopsis of Christian Theology**, Edgar C. Barton, 25-35 City Road, E.C.I. London, The Epworth Press.

15. Pearlman, Myer, **Knowing the Doctrines of the Bible**, Springfield, Missouri, Gospel Publishing House, 1945.

16. Pieper, Francis, D. D., **Christian Dogmatics**, Saint Louis, Missouri, Concordia Publishing House, 1953.

17. Pink, Arthur W., **An Exposition of Hebrews**, Grand Rapids, Michigan, Baker Book House, 1971.

18. Prince, Derek, B.A., M.A., **From Jordan to Pentecost**, P.O. Box 306, Fort Lauderdale, Florida 33302.

19. Strong, James, **Exhaustive Concordance**, New Jersey, Madison, 1890.

20. Tappert, Theodore G., **The Book of Concord**, Confessions of the Evangelical Lutheran Church, Philadelphia, Fortress Press, 1959.

21. Thayer, Joseph Henry, D. D., **Thayer's Greek-English Lexicon**, Grand Rapids, Michigan, Associated Publishers & Authors Inc.

22. Thiessen, Henry C., **Lectures in Systematic Theology**, Grand Rapids, Michigan, Wm. B. Eerdmans Publishing Co., 1963.

23. Thompson, Frank Charles, **The New Chain Reference Bible**, Indianapolis, Indiana, B. B. Kirkbride Bible Co. Inc., 164.

24. Trench, Richard Chenevit, D. D., **Synonyms of the New Testament**, Grand Rapids, Michigan, Associated Publishers & Authors Inc.

25. Unger, Merrill F., Th.D. Ph.D., Chicago, **Unger's Bible Dictionary**, Chicago, Moody Press, 1972

26. Vine, W. E., **An Expository Dictionary of the New Testament Words**, Old Tappan, New Jersey, Fleming H. Revell Company, 1966.

27. Walker, Williston, **A History of the Christian Church**, New York, Charles Scribner's Sons, 1970.

28. White, R. E. O., M.A., B.D., **The Biblical Doctrine of Initiation**, Grand Rapids, Michigan, Wm. B. Eerdmans Publishing Company, 1960.

29. William Arndt & F. Wilbur Gingrich, **A Greek-English Lexicon of the New Testament** & Other Early Christian Literature, Chicago, University of Chicago Press, 1969.

30. Young, Robert, LL.D., **Analytical Concordance to the Holy Bible**, United Society for Christian Literature, Lutterworth Press, London, 1953.

Other Books by Kevin Conner

The Kingdom Cult of Self

Kings of the Kingdom

Law and Grace

The Lord Jesus Christ our Melchizedek Priest

The Manifest Presence (NEW)

Marriage, Divorce and Remarriage

Methods and Principles of Bible Research

Ministries in the Cluster

The Ministry of Women

Mystery Parables of the Kingdom

The Name of God

New Covenant Realities

Only for Catholics

Passion Week Chart

Psalms - A Commentary

The Relevance of the Old Testament to a New Testament Church

Restoration Theology

Romans (An Exposition)

The Seventy Weeks Prophecy

The Sword and Consequences

The Tabernacle of David

The Tabernacle of Moses

The Temple of Solomon

Table Talks

Tale of Three Trees

This is My Story (Kevin Conner's best-selling autobiography)

This We Believe

Three Days and Three Nights (with Chart)

Tithes and Offerings

Today's Prophets

To Drink or Not to Drink

To Smoke or Not to Smoke

Understanding the New Birth and the Baptism of the Holy Spirit

Vision of an Antioch Church

Water Baptism Thesis

What About Israel? (NEW)

Visit www.kevinconner.org for more information.

Visit www.amazon.com for a list of Kevin Conner's books available on Kindle.

Made in the USA
Coppell, TX
23 May 2023

17196611R00046